Contsting the sacred

Contesting the Sacred undertakes a major re-think of earlier anthropological studies of Christian pilgrimage, notably *Image and Pilgrimage in Christian Culture* (V. and E. Turner), the most influential book in its field. This new study explores the limitations of the Turnerian perspective within the context of recent debates and developments in anthropology and sociology.

The contributors, who all have detailed knowledge of the complexity of Christian pilgrimage, propose a new agenda for pilgrimage studies, recognizing above all that pilgrimage is an arena for competing religious and secular discourses. Their investigations highlight the heterogeneity of the pilgrimage process, and their descriptive and analytical accounts provide a valuable basis for comparing different Christian shrines across the world. Particular shrines in France, Italy, Israel, Sri Lanka and Peru are examined with regard not only to the dynamics of religious expression and belief, but also the political and economic processes operating at local and more global levels.

This new theoretical approach to the sacred in general and pilgrimage in particular links up with general developments within anthropology and suggests ways forward in the analysis of pilgrimage. *Contesting the Sacred* will appeal to students and teachers of anthropology, sociology, theology and religious studies, history, and social and cultural geography.

John Eade is Senior Lecturer in the Department of Sociology and Social Administration at Roehampton Institute, London. The late **Michael J. Sallnow** was Senior Lecturer in Social Anthropology at the London School of Economics.

Contesting the sacred
The anthropology of Christian pilgrimage

Edited by
John Eade
and
Michael J. Sallnow

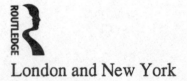

London and New York

First published 1991
by Routledge
11 New Fetter Lane, London EC4P 4EE

Simultaneously published in the USA and Canada
by Routledge
a division of Routledge, Chapman and Hall, Inc.
29 West 35th Street, New York, NY 10001

Typeset by Michael Mepham, Frome, Somerset
Printed and bound in Great Britain by Mackays of Chatham PLC,
Chatham, Kent

British Library Cataloguing in Publication Data
Contesting the sacred : the anthropology of Christian
    pilgrimage.
    1. Christian pilgrimage – Sociological perspectives
    I. Eade, John   II. Sallnow, Michael J.
    306.6

Library of Congress Cataloging in Publication Data
Contesting the sacred : the anthropology of Christian
    pilgrimage / edited by John Eade and Michael J. Sallnow.
    p.   cm.
    Includes bibliographical references and index.
    1. Christian pilgrims and pilgrimages.
    2. Turner, Victor Witter. Image and pilgrimage in Christian
    culture.   I. Eade, John, 1946–.
    II. Sallnow, Michael J., 1949–1991.
    BX2323.C59   1991
    306.6'48463–dc20   90-36733
                                                        CIP

ISBN 0-415-04360-3
ISBN 0-415-04361-1 (pbk)

To the memory of Michael J. Sallnow, 1949–1990

Contents

Figures

Contributors

Glenn Bowman is a Lecturer in Communications and Image Studies at the University of Kent. He has undertaken research in Israel on Christian Arabs and is completing his doctoral thesis at the University of Oxford. He has published several articles concerning Israeli nationalism and tourism and plans to return to Israel to study the transmission of Christian identity in a situation of revolution.

Andrea Dahlberg completed her doctoral thesis on pilgrimage to Lourdes at the London School of Economics, University of London, after undergraduate training in Australia and post-graduate courses at the University of London. She was appointed as a Research Fellow at Brunel University and her research interests concern the notion of incorporation in Christianity and British law.

John Eade is Senior Lecturer in Sociology and Social Anthropology at the Roehampton Institute, London. He has undertaken research on the Bengali Muslim minority in Calcutta as well as a study of the politics of Bangladeshi community representation in London's East End. He has worked for over twenty years as a helper at Lourdes.

Christopher McKevitt completed his doctoral thesis on Padre Pio's shrine at San Giovanni Rotondo at the London School of Economics after an undergraduate degree at Victoria University, Wellington (New Zealand). He is now based at the Academic Department of Community Medicine, St Mary's Hospital Medical School, London.

Michael J. Sallnow was Senior Lecturer in Social Anthropology at the London School of Economics.

Richard L. Stirrat teaches social anthropology at the University of Sussex. He has undertaken extensive research into Catholic pilgrimage in Sri Lanka and has published a number of articles based on his fieldwork during the last ten years. He is currently completing a monograph on Catholics in Sri Lanka.

Foreword

Although its doctrinal status varies considerably, pilgrimage is an important institution in all the world religions. Those previous studies which, explicitly or implicitly, adopted a sociological approach tended to interpret pilgrimage as either supporting or as subverting the established social order. With Christian pilgrimage as its focus, this book seeks to break that rather limiting mould. It proposes a new agenda which would deconstruct pilgrimage and see it as a phenomenon combining both these opposing tendencies in an arena of competing religious and secular discourses, rival orthodoxies, sects and confessional groupings. Thus, in Christian pilgrimage, as the following chapters document, there is generally a pervasive tension between the stress on redemption of the official religious discourse, and the less other-worldly discourse of the pilgrims themselves which tends to focus on healing and help in present extremities. This contradiction is to some extent resolved in the traditional Catholic view of pilgrimage as a form of penance and as a meritorious act (cf. pilgrimage to Mecca in Islam).

The multi-dimensional view of the meaning of pilgrimage advocated here also prompts John Eade and Michael Sallnow to develop a more satisfactory analytical typology of pilgrimage itself. As they argue, and *pace* Eliade, pilgrimage is not only a matter of visiting designated sacred places and shrines. Pilgrims also throng to seek the blessing of particular holy men – sacred persons who in certain periods and settings may challenge the power of long-established shrines. Historically, it might be argued, sacred persons and sacred shrines constitute phases in a developmental sequence of pilgrimage power since death and canonization transform the former into the latter. Be that as it may, as the editors point out, whether addressed to specific holy men or to particular holy places, pilgrimage stimulates economic as well as religious transactions in a wider system of exchange. It might be added that, not only as trade centres, but also as cultural and inter-cultural bazaars, such centres of exchange play an extremely important role in the diffusion and re-diffusion of all kinds of ideas and practices. They may thus contribute to the spread of unorthodox, not to say dissident, as well as orthodox customs, concurrently supporting and challenging the official cult.

Recognition of this again underlines the value of the pluralist model of pilgrimage so forcefully advocated by John Eade and Michael Sallnow in this stimulating book which will, I am sure, mark an important new development in pilgrimage studies and encourage much discussion and debate, and not only in relation to Christian pilgrimage. It is sad that Michael Sallnow who died in May 1990 did not live to see the publication of this fine book. Nevertheless, desperately ill though he was, he managed to correct his set of the proofs and thus had the satisfaction of bestowing his seal on a work which, taken together with his outstanding monograph *Pilgrims of the Andes* (1987), constitutes an important and innovative contribution to the anthropological study of religion.

I. M. Lewis
London, 10 July 1990

Acknowledgements

This book is the product of a close collaboration between Mike Sallnow and myself, which was sadly ended by Mike's premature death in May 1990. Mike and I wrote different sections of the draft editorial introduction but the final version is in Mike's inimitable hand. He was also indefatigable in the preparation of the other chapters for the publishers. Given his personal circumstances during 1989 his commitment to the book was an inspiration. His fortitude, careful attention to detail and sensitivity to others are the qualities which particularly impressed me during the preparation of a publication which will, I hope, stand as a lasting testament to his contribution to the field of pilgrimage studies.

I would also like to thank the other contributors for their co-operation. Andrea Dahlberg was especially helpful when it came to choosing a title for the book and revising my chapter on Lourdes. Jean Canfield and her colleagues at the London School of Economics provided invaluable support during the typing of the chapter and I am very grateful to Professor Ieuan Lewis for so willingly and promptly contributing a Foreword. Thanks are also due to Heather Gibson and Lynda Goldman at Routledge for their calm professionalism during the preparation of the manuscript and to Dr Richard Werbner for the enthusiastic welcome and helpful comments which he gave to my initial proposal.

The stimulus for the book came from a conference which I organized in 1988 and I am grateful to all those who contributed papers. I benefited greatly from the support and interest of my colleagues, especially Dr Peter Hughes and Dr Tom Selwyn, my friends – Dr Lis Cook in particular – and the members of the various pilgrimages to Lourdes, especially those in the Oxford University Catholic Chaplaincy Pilgrimage. Finally, although they bear no responsibility for my interpretation of Lourdes I would like to thank Fr David Forrester for introducing me to the shrine and Fr Michael Hollings for his inspirational leadership.

Introduction

John Eade and Michael J. Sallnow

This book has its origins in a conference on pilgrimage convened by John Eade at the Roehampton Institute of Higher Education in July 1988. The conference was interdisciplinary, embracing social anthropologists, sociologists, historians, and theologians, and the twenty-four papers dealt with pilgrimage in a variety of religious traditions.

Faced with the task of selecting a manageable number of chapters to form a coherent comparative collection, the editors chose to adopt two main criteria. It was decided that the dominant disciplinary orientation should be anthropological, as for the most part, it was these chapters that went 'on the offensive', so to speak, in attempting to set a new agenda for the study of pilgrimage.[1] It was also decided that the book should be restricted to the Christian tradition, broadly defined, partly because the majority of conference papers fell within this area, partly because, when dealing with such a broad topic, comparison is more fruitful if at least some of the parameters are held constant. Furthermore, the burgeoning literature on the anthropology of Christianity makes a book dedicated to Christian pilgrimage particularly timely.

These chapters, in fact, capture Christian pilgrimage in a variety of historical moments and cultural conjunctions. The circum-Mediterranean area, as the heartland of the Christian tradition, is the dominant geographical focus. Jerusalem, the subject of Bowman's chapter, was the first true pilgrimage site of Christendom, consciously created as such by the emperor Constantine to provide a physical anchorage for the written texts of the newly adopted state religion with which he hoped to unify the empire. Today, however, Jerusalem stands as a kind of microcosm of all the antagonistic creeds, sects, and denominations into which the Judaeo-Christian tradition has splintered over the centuries. In sharp contrast, San Giovanni Rotondo, described in the chapter by McKevitt, is one of the newest pilgrimage locations, transformed in the last few decades from a sleepy backwater in southern Italy to an international holy centre thanks to the presence, in life and in death, of a stigmatized Capuchin friar.

The two complementary chapters by Dahlberg and Eade focus on Lourdes, perhaps the best-known of Catholic pilgrimage shrines. Lourdes has its origins in that genre of the miraculous familiar since late medieval times, the Marian apparition. At the same time, however, it belongs very much to the present epoch, emerging out of the particular historical circumstances of nineteenth-century France and co-opted by the church to affirm papal authority and the ascendancy of spiritual over secular, rationalist values in the modern world.

The chapters by Stirrat and Sallnow, meanwhile, take us beyond the Christian heartland, with familiar themes and forms reappearing in guises superficially recognizable but, in reality, radically transformed. Both Sri Lanka and Peru, the two countries with which these chapters deal, were proselytized by Catholic missionaries in the sixteenth century. But the respective colonial contexts which determined the pattern of development of the imported religion, its nexus with the dominant secular powers, and its relationship with indigenous cultural traditions, differed profoundly. In Sri Lanka, Christianity remained the religion of a minority – albeit a privileged minority – enclaved within the dominant Sinhalese Buddhist culture. In the Andes, the imperial cults of the Inkas were eliminated, and Christianity assumed the role of the new state religion; but local indigenous cults persisted, and became intimately interwoven with the new Christian observances.

In the Sri Lankan case, then, Catholicism has operated within the shadow of another, deeply rooted 'great tradition', possessed of texts and literati and closely bound up with a nationalist political consciousness. In the case of Peru, Catholicism has established political hegemony but has been subverted, so to speak, by the local indigenous religion of an illiterate peasantry. In each case, the character of pilgrimage and of its focal shrines reflects these contrasting historical configurations.

What, then, is the new agenda in pilgrimage studies that emerges from these chapters? Put briefly, it amounts to a recognition that pilgrimage is above all an arena for competing religious and secular discourses, for both the official co-optation and the non-official recovery of religious meanings, for conflict between orthodoxies, sects, and confessional groups, for drives towards consensus and communitas, *and* for counter-movements towards separateness and division. The essential heterogeneity of the pilgrimage process, which was marginalized or suppressed in the earlier, deterministic models of both the correspondence theorists and those who adopted a Turnerian paradigm, is here pushed centre-stage, rendered problematic. As a direct consequence, the theoretical discourse *about* pilgrimage becomes more diversified and discrepant, being less concerned to match empirical instances with a preconceived ideal – whether analytically or theologically inspired – than to deconstruct the very category of 'pilgrimage' into historically and culturally specific behaviours and meanings. For, if one can no longer take for granted the meaning of a pilgrimage for its participants, one can no longer take for granted a uniform definition of the phenomenon of 'pilgrimage' either.

CORRESPONDENCE THEORY AND TURNER'S PARADIGM

The new directions in pilgrimage studies mapped out by the contributors to this volume can be best appreciated against the background of earlier, structuralist modes of interpretation of the phenomenon. It was perhaps inevitable that a discipline founded upon the study of small-scale, non-western societies, one that quite properly stressed the organizational coherence and cultural integration of such societies as against popular misconceptions of primitive anarchy and infantilism, should come to replicate these overly functionalist biases when it turned its attention to wider and more extensive groupings and gatherings. In fact, of course, the idea of the great religious festival as social unifier and moral regenerator had already been set forth in Durkheim's classic text *The Elementary Forms of the Religious Life* in 1912, during the formative years of social and cultural anthropology; and, flawed though it was,[2] Durkheim's characterization of Australian Aboriginal ritual came to provide a convenient paradigm for the anthropological analysis of supra-local religious cults.

Accordingly, many writers on pilgrimage have perceived the activity as a crucial operator which welds together diverse local communities and social strata into more extensive collectivities. Pilgrimages have tended to be treated as local cults writ large, though at the same time they are seen as offsetting or complementing the introversion of such cults, by instilling in the participants a consciousness of a wider and more inclusive identity. Such an identity might be regional or tribal, as in Spiro's study of Buddhist pilgrimage in Burma (1970), Rabinow's of Berber pilgrimage in Morocco (1975), or Marx's of Bedouin pilgrimage in Sinai (1977). Or the pilgrimage might foster a nationalist consciousness, as Wolf has argued for the cult of the Virgin of Guadalupe in Mexico (1958), Fought for the cult of Christ of Esquipulas in Guatemala (1969), Obeyesekere for Buddhist centres in Sri Lanka (1966), and Cohn and Marriott for Hindu shrines in India (1958). Or the integrative function of pilgrimage might be seen as operating at the level of the civilization as a whole, the cults being viewed as crucial media for disseminating religious orthodoxy amongst the unlettered masses, as in the hierarchical formulations of Redfield (1956) and Srinivas (1967).[3]

This Durkheimian approach to pilgrimage is sometimes given a Marxist slant. Here, the cults are implicated in the generation and maintenance of ideologies which legitimize domination and oppression. For example, Gross argues that the relationship between pilgrim and shrine divinity in the cult of Bom Jesus da Lapa in north-eastern Brazil has the effect of sacralizing the earthly patron–client relationship between peasants and their political superiors (1971). Similarly, Eickelman sees Islamic pilgrimage in Morocco as preserving and legitimizing secular inequalities in the wider society (1976).

The alternative formulation proposed by Victor Turner (Turner 1974a, 1974b; Turner and Turner 1978), based mainly on studies of pilgrimage in the Christian tradition, stands in direct counterpoint to these functionalist, correspondence theories. Pilgrimage for Turner, so far from reflecting or reinforcing secular social structure, is a liminal phenomenon which betokens the partial, if not complete, abrogation of that structure. Pilgrimage, being stereotypically focused on powerful but peripheral shrines commanding widespread recognition and devotion, is *anti*-structural: it always tends towards communitas, a state of unmediated and egalitarian association between individuals who are temporarily freed of the hierarchical secular roles and statuses which they bear in everyday life. The achievement of communitas is the pilgrim's fundamental motivation. Logistical and organizational imperatives invariably compromise this goal, however, and in practice structure reasserts itself in the pilgrimage context to a greater or lesser degree. Nevertheless, because pilgrimage cults are essentially inclusive and universalistic, the tendency towards communitas will always be discernible. Pilgrimage, in other words, to the degree that it strips actors of their social personae and restores their essential individuality, is the ritual context *par excellence* in which a world religion strives to realize its defining transcultural universalism; for to reach the individual is to reach the universal.[4]

Turner's model has been subjected to a number of theoretical critiques (Werbner 1977; Morinis 1984; Sallnow 1987) and has been tested in a variety of field settings – Morocco (Eickelman 1976), Nepal (Messerschmidt and Sharma 1981), Sri Lanka (Pfaffenberger 1979), West Bengal (Morinis 1984), north India (Van der Veer 1984) and the Peruvian Andes (Sallnow 1981). In none of these cases did the investigator find support for the theory; to the contrary, a recurrent theme throughout the literature is the maintenance and, in many instances, the reinforcement of social boundaries and distinctions in the pilgrimage context, rather than their attenuation or dissolution. This is not to say, of course, that some of the features and conditions glossed by the term 'communitas' will not be found in some cases. As the theoretical critiques show, however, it is the determinism of the model which limits its usefulness, for the necessary alignment of pilgrimage and anti-structure not only prejudges the complex character of the phenomenon but also imposes a spurious homogeneity on the practice of pilgrimage in widely differing historical and cultural settings.

Despite the positivism of the one and the dialectical pretensions of the other, the functionalist and Turnerian approaches share the same structuralist foundations, with pilgrimage being seen as either supporting or subverting the established social order. In order to transcend this somewhat simplistic dichotomy, it is necessary to develop a view of pilgrimage not merely as a field of social relations but also as a *realm of competing discourses*. Indeed, much of what Turner has to say could be seen as representative of a particular discourse *about* pilgrimage rather than as an empirical description *of* it, one which might well co-exist or compete with alternative discourses. It is these varied discourses with their multiple meanings and understandings, brought to the shrine by different categories of pilgrims, by residents and by religious specialists, that are constitutive of the cult itself. Equally, a cult might be seen to be constituted by mutual *mis*understandings, as each group attempts to interpret the actions and motives of others in terms of its own specific discourse.

Accordingly, the analytical emphasis shifts from positivist, generic accounts of the features and functions of pilgrimage, and of the extrinsic characteristics of its focal shrines, towards an investigation of how the practice of pilgrimage and the sacred powers of a shrine are constructed as varied and possibly conflicting representations by the different sectors of the cultic constituency, and indeed by those outside it as well. This, in essence, is the starting point for the papers in this symposium. In the remainder of this introduction, we highlight the principal arguments of the contributors, and explore them thematically in a comparative perspective.

DECONSTRUCTING THE CENTRE

Let us consider, to begin with, the very *raison d'être* of pilgrimage, the notion of a 'holy place'. For Eliade, whose writings heavily influenced Turner's work, every pilgrimage shrine is an archetype of a sacred centre, marked off from the profane space surrounding it, where heaven and earth intersect and where time stands still, where there exists the possibility of breaking through to the realm of the transcendent (Eliade 1963). This does approximate to what is sometimes encountered in certain religious discourses, as Eliade demonstrates. But such a rarefied generalization suppresses the quite profound differences in the ways in which holy places are conceptualized from instance to instance, and sometimes within the same instance.

A pilgrimage locale is typically a site associated either with the manifestation of the divine to human beings or with the human propensity to approach the divine. At Lourdes, for example, the little grotto where the Virgin Mary appeared to Bernadette Soubirous became a fount of sacred power which continues to manifest itself through the eyes of pilgrims in occasional miraculous cures. Here, place, and the power of place, are clearly paramount. In the Andes, which fell under the influence of Catholicism at a time when miraculous, apparitional shrines were very much in vogue in Europe, there would seem to be an analogous connection between sites of theophanies of the Virgin and Christ on the one hand, and miraculous powers of healing on the other. Yet there are in the Andes at least two quite different perspectives on a miraculous shrine as a sacred place. In one perspective, the shrine can be seen as emanating directly from the matrix of an animate landscape: it is a special instance of the chthonic powers of the terrain, which elsewhere work through the mountain lords and the other spirit owners of nature. But in another perspective, it can be seen as the consecration of the territory via random apparitions by external, foreign divinities, whose power is *sui generis* but who choose to channel it through particular sites to particular populations. Certain kinds of mythic discourse can be seen as an attempt to reconcile these two opposed conceptions, by portraying the shrines as the petrified bodies of wandering gods, their power emanating from their still-living bodies.

Here, though, the mythic discourse registers a shift in the notion of sacred centre, from a purely *place*-centred sacredness to one having to do with the inherent sanctity of a holy *person* – albeit, in this case, the person of a mythic divinity. In other cases elsewhere in the ethnography, spatial sacredness gives way entirely to the bodily holiness of a living focal personality, the saintly mortal or god incarnate. In the new wave of Christian shrines in Sri Lanka, for example, it is the living body of the saint that exudes sacred power, rather than a physical location as in the older, more established shrines in the region. If a sacred centre offers the opportunity for direct contact with the divine, then relocating that centre in a human body makes the divine even more accessible and responsive to human needs and aspirations.

Stirrat interprets the shift of devotional interest from the older, place-specific shrines to the new person-centred cults primarily in terms of the pervasive role of patronage in Sri Lankan politics and social life. The charismatic cult leaders, actively invoking particular saints to salve the misfortunes of their devotees, are the religious counterparts of powerful political patrons in the secular domain: they personalize the divine just as members of parliament personalize the state. Indeed, the holy men of the Sinhala Catholics embody what the MPs desire: the infusion of the divine which will make them unique.

The shift from place-centred to person-centred sacredness, however, does not always rest upon a secular, political model; in some cases, it is a matter of independent transformation *within* the religious domain itself, albeit one that may be stimulated by other processes outside the cults. Such an example is mentioned in the chapter by Sallnow – the sixteenth-century Andean millenarian movement known as the Taki Onqoy, literally 'dancing sickness'. Here, thirty years after the Spanish conquest, the native gods which had hitherto been localized in features of the natural landscape became relocated in the bodies of adepts, whose dance-trances provided a direct medium of communication with the neglected indigenous deities. Their message was the defeat of the Christian pantheon and the rise of a new humanity in the Andes. In this case, the shift from place-centred to person-centred cults was provoked by the crisis of conquest, for possessed individuals are able to respond more rapidly and effectively to changing needs and events than are static shrines embedded in the landscape – particularly when, as in this case, there were no longer any priests to interpret their oracular pronouncements.

Today, living saints pose considerable problems for a centralized, bureaucratic religious instititution like the Catholic church, for they obviate altogether the need for priestly intermediaries. The personification of the sacred centre is a movement to the limits of ecclesiastical control, a control which begins to be regained only with the death of the saint and his or her transformation into a mute, hieratic, domesticated shrine.

Such a transformation is illustrated in McKevitt's chapter on the Italian cult of Padre Pio, the Capuchin friar whose body bore the wounds of the crucified Christ and whose suffering has been a source of inspiration for pilgrims drawn from far afield. In this case, the aura of holiness which emanated from the person of Padre Pio in life is being gradually trans- muted into a spatial sacredness anchored in the places he frequented and sanctified by his presence. A sacred geography is being etched into the landscape around the crypt in which his body lies, comprising the various locations which most strongly evoke his spirit – for example, the place where he first received the stigmata, his cell, and his confessional. To paraphrase Weber, we might call this process the 'spatialization of char- isma': the power of the living person is sedimented and preserved after his death in the power of place. Furthermore, for the devotees of Padre Pio at least, the entire region has become a geographical microcosm of the moral universe, with the intense holiness of the friary and shrine counterposed to the profane and even satanic character of the adjacent village of San Giovanni Rotondo. Space has become charged with relig- ious meaning, to the extent that some pilgrims directly equate the locality with the area around Mount Calvary in the Holy Land, where Christ himself met his death.

Place-centred sacredness, then, besides being capable of construction in quite different ways, is but one modality of the localization of divine power encountered in pilgrimage cults. Person-centred sacredness might precede it empirically, as in the case of Padre Pio, or might arise in counterpoint to it, as in the examples of modern Sri Lanka and the sixteenth-century Andes. But there is yet another modality, in which the sacred centre becomes more abstract and rarefied than in either of these two, materialized centricities: the location of divine power not in a person, nor in a place, but in a *text*. Jerusalem, the focus of Bowman's chapter, provides a prime example of what might be called 'textual pilgrimage'.

Christian pilgrimage to Jerusalem is, in one perspective, a spiritual recovery of Christ via the places where he walked, preached, suffered, and died. Yet because of this intimate connection with Christ's biography, it has always been not just, or even primarily, a journey to particular locations, but more importantly a journey through a particular written text, the authorized, biblical accounts of Christ's life and death. Modern Roman Catholic pilgrimage to Jerusalem, for example, is similarly a movement through a series of texts, recited by the group leader at the appropriate sites, with the holy places threaded into an itinerary which fleshes out and gives facticity to the biography of Christ as reported in the gospels. Moreover, it is the significance of what happened at these various sites, and the lessons to be learned thereby for leading a Christian life, that are of primary importance for the pilgrims. Indeed, pilgrimage sites around Jerusalem can be moved and re-established with no loss of sacred or pedagogical significance, for the same text is merely mapped on to the new locations. For Roman Catholics at least, the purpose of pilgrimage to Jerusalem is, in a sense, to verify and materialize the sacred scriptures, to make them real, and to extract the maximum instructional content from them, rather than to visit the sites *per se*.

For the Catholic pilgrim to Jerusalem, then – and as Bowman shows, one must be careful to distinguish Catholics from other Christian denominations in this respect – the sacred geography is relevant only in so far as it illustrates an authoritative text. Indeed, one could go so far as to say that the holy places of Jerusalem radiate no power as such – it is significant that no miraculous healing qualities are associated with them, nor are penitential practices engaged in to tap their sacredness. They are visited as illustrations of a text that is itself the ultimate source of power. Paradoxically, for the pilgrimage to the very cradle of Christianity, to the haunts of Christ himself, the power of person and the power of place recede against the far greater power of the word.

The sacred centre, then, can assume many different forms. The thrust of our analytic endeavour should be not towards the formulation of ever more inclusive, and consequently ever more vacuous, generalizations, but instead towards the examination of the specific peculiarities of its construction in each instance. We suggest that the triad of 'person', 'place', and 'text' might provide the co-ordinates for this task as far as Christian pilgrimage is concerned, and perhaps for pilgrimage in other scripturally based religious traditions as well.

PERCEPTIONS OF THE SACRED

The traditional, Eliadean notion of the sacred centre which has tended to permeate the literature on pilgrimage throws up another, more fundamental problem. In the conventional view, the power of a miraculous shrine is seen to derive solely from its inherent capacity to exert a devotional magnetism over pilgrims from far and wide, and to exude of itself potent meanings and significances for its worshippers. The shrine is seen, so to speak, as *sui generis*: its power is internally generated and its meanings are largely predetermined.

All the contributors to this symposium implicitly or explicitly contest this view. What their various analyses suggest is that a pilgrimage shrine, while apparently emanating an intrinsic religious significance of its own, at the same time provides a ritual space for the expression of a diversity of perceptions and meanings which the pilgrims themselves bring to the shrine and impose upon it. As such, the cult can contain within itself a plethora of religious discourses. For McKevitt, there are at least two Padre Pios, that of the devotees and that of the townspeople; for Bowman, there are as many Jerusalems as there are religious denominations visiting the city. As well as perhaps being a symbolic power-house productive of its own religious meanings, a pilgrimage shrine is also – sometimes predominantly – an arena for the interplay of a variety of imported perceptions and understandings, in some cases finely differentiated from one another, in others radically polarized.

With regard to Lourdes, for example, many of the pilgrims perceive the shrine in terms of what Dahlberg labels a 'miracle discourse'. They come in pursuit of divine favour, of some tangible sign that God and the Virgin have their various individual interests at heart. Other pilgrims, together with the majority of the senior shrine staff, on the other hand, tend to operate with a quite different kind of discourse. For them, the act of pilgrimage is pre-eminently a sacrifice, a replay on a lesser scale of Christ's own sacrifice on the cross. Miracles might occur, but they should not be regarded as the central purpose of the activity.

These two discourses compete, on somewhat unequal terms, for supremacy in the cult. As Dahlberg points out, Lourdes has long been an important evangelizing centre under the central direction of Rome: the cult was promoted initially to rebut secular rationalism and to assert the authority of the papacy. More recently, pilgrims have been encouraged to support the reforms initiated by the Second Vatican Council through their participation in new rituals and procedures. Officials might be expected, therefore, to exercise considerable control over the ways in which pilgrims interpret the meaning of Lourdes and express themselves in public ritual.

Yet the continuing co-existence of the two discourses indicates that the power of official reformers is nevertheless still constrained by traditions to which lay pilgrims, and some priests, remain strongly attached. The shrine officials do not in fact constitute a solidary group exerting a totalitarian power. The situation is complex, with pilgrims being able occasionally to impose their own meanings on situations and to pursue non-official practices – albeit within the constraints of the pilgrimage and shrine organizations.

Eade's chapter provides a concrete, micro-sociological example of the manner in which pilgrims are, to a limited extent, able to wield their own power to pursue ritual practices in defiance of the wishes of shrine officials, in this case the Hospitallers who supervise the bathing of pilgrims. To a degree, the pilgrims are able to shape the bathing process – for many of them, especially the sick, the rationale of the entire pilgrimage – according to their own designs, designs which might be informed by a discourse quite at odds with the authoritative version and its prescribed procedures. Furthermore, some officials, especially those at the lower levels of the Hospitality hierarchy who occupy an ambiguous position between their pilgrim charges and the senior lay and priestly officials, occasionally ally themselves with pilgrims in defiance of received practices.

Nevertheless, the freedom of pilgrims is tightly qualified. The officials are frequently able to impose their own definitions of the situation, despite the pilgrims' resistance. Moreover, their control over the organization of space and time in relation to shrine activities gives officials a considerable advantage over pilgrims in imposing conformity on ritual activities.

Even so, the definition and bounding of sacred space is contested by some pilgrims. Officials tend to protect sacred objects and areas from those not specifically validated by the shrine authorities. However, many pilgrims do not appear to have the same notion of the vulnerability of the sacred, and they frequently attempt to break down the official boundary between secular and sacred space in order to be as close as possible to the transcendent.

Lourdes, because of its careful guardianship by the church since its inception, is perhaps the most tightly controlled and orchestrated, at the levels of both meaning and practice, of all the pilgrimage cults considered in this volume. Other cases present different scenarios of the confrontation between official power and devotional resistance. In Sri Lanka, the new breakaway cults have escaped from ecclesiastical control altogether, thereby giving free rein to alternative discourses about sickness, healing, and sacred power. The charismatic individuals who are the foci of these cults embody a divine power which is in no way dependent on the church. Somewhat paradoxically, however, advocates of the new shrines have sought legitimation through the claim that it is through these individuals that the divine has chosen to intervene in order to persuade the laity to return to the true, traditional Catholicism.

In the Andes, meanwhile, many cults contain within themselves the tensions and contradictions of an official Catholic devotionalism confronting so-called 'popular' religious meanings and practices. During the colonial period, as Sallnow shows, Indians and Spaniards interpreted the spate of miraculous apparitions of Christ and the Virgin in diametrically opposite ways, and today conflicting perceptions are still imported to pilgrimage shrines by Indians and *mestizos*[5] respectively. The confrontation thereby acquires an ethnic cast, being perceived in terms of an orthodox, Hispanic religiosity versus a paganized, indigenous variant. Thus, at the shrine of Señor de Wank'a, the ritual dances of Indian pilgrims were proscribed by the Mercedarian priests,[6] who were attempting to incline the devotion towards a more orthodox form of piety.

However, other 'popular' practices such as self-flagellation still persist: despite their unease at such activities, the priests are powerless to prevent them. Indeed, at another important shrine in the Cusco region, Señor de Qoyllur Rit'i, the lay brotherhood which controls the shrine is actually empowered to inflict ceremonial whippings on pilgrims, either at the behest of the pilgrim as a form of penance or as punishment for some minor solecism or ritual infraction. Again, the priests in attendance are obliged to accept such behaviour, though many clearly disapprove. In this case, the whip is an obvious symbol of the power of the lay brotherhood over the pilgrims, and of their control over the religious discourse and ritual procedures at the shrine. Some groups of pilgrims, however, have found a simple way of evading the power of these officials: by opting out of certain procedures altogether and merely paying a brief visit to the sanctuary, staying in the shrine precincts for as short a time as possible.

These contradictions between official and non-official discourses, and conflicts between shrine custodians and shrine devotees, derive ultimately from differing perceptions of the holy place itself. The chapters by McKevitt and Bowman focus explicitly on this issue. It is a commonplace in the literature that people who live in the vicinity of an important shrine rarely visit it, preferring instead to make pilgrimage to shrines further afield. This is typically attributed to the devotional necessity of arduous travel as a form of penance in order to make the invocation of divine power effective. The great value of McKevitt's chapter is that it goes beyond such superficial interpretation to examine, in a specific instance, the complex and ambivalent attitudes of locals towards a nearby shrine and its cult.

For the Sangiovannesi, the shrine on the outskirts of their town is a centre not only of sacred power, radiating from the remains of Padre Pio, but more importantly of secular power, represented by the outsiders – the doctors and administrators at the hospital which Pio founded, and the resident devotees – who now inhabit the suburb. But whereas, during his lifetime, Padre Pio interceded effectively on behalf of the Sangiovannesi to secure political and material benefits for the town, since his death the feeling of local residents is that they have been excluded both from the secular benefits bestowed by Pio and also from the sacred aspect of his legacy, which has been compromised and complicated through its appropriation by 'fanatical' outsiders.

To the profound resentment of the Sangiovannesi, then, the twin powers of the shrine have passed out of their control. The sacred locale on their doorstep, originally the site of their 'own' miraculous image of the Madonna and more recently the residence of a man who in effect acted as their exclusive political patron, has become almost alien, peopled by foreigners and controlled by organizations, secular and ecclesiastical, for whom the interests of the Sangiovannesi are of little account. The town has been entirely marginalized by the holy place it spawned. As already mentioned, the perception of some of the resident devotees towards the Sangiovannesi reciprocates this negative image but translates it into a religious idiom: because of their apparent indifference towards the shrine, the townspeople are seen as diabolic, symptomatic of the devil-ridden, sinful world from which the shrine of Padre Pio offers an escape.

The clash of conflicting perceptions of a sacred locale is further illustrated by the multi-denominational pilgrimages to Jerusalem. Here, Judaism, Islam, and a variety of Christianities jostle with one another in an atmosphere of deep suspicion and sometimes outright hostility. Bowman shows how each group brings to Jerusalem its own interpretation of the city as a sacred location. Jerusalem provides a contrast with Lourdes, San Giovanni Rotondo, and the Andean and Sri Lankan cases in that the conflicting definitions of sacred power invested in its holy places are not restricted to those of officials versus pilgrims, or indigenes versus outsiders, but are ultimately related to far more complex sectarian, interdenominational, and international antagonisms, which come to be played out in terms of competition for ritual space and time within a tightly circumscribed religious arena. The process of validating Jerusalem and the Holy Land generally is thus intimately bound up with political and ideological conflict at both national and international levels.

Bowman provides detailed descriptions and analyses of three contrasting Christian pilgrimages – Greek Orthodox, Roman Catholic, and Christian Zionist. He demonstrates convincingly that each group brings to Jerusalem their own entrenched understandings of the sacred; nothing unites them save their mere sequential – and sometimes simultaneous –

presence at the same holy sites. For the Greek Orthodox pilgrims, indeed, the precise identification of the site itself is largely irrelevant; it is the icons on display which are the principal focus of attention. For the Roman Catholics, as already mentioned, the site is important in that it is illustrative of a particular biblical text relating to the life of Jesus; but it is important only in a historical sense, as confirming the truth of past events. Only for the Christian Zionists does the Holy Land itself carry any present and future significance, and here they find a curious kinship with indigenous Jews. Even between three Christian denominations, then, the gulfs in the perceptions of the holy places of Jerusalem are vast, surpassing any kind of compromise or mutual understanding. The sacred centre *par excellence* of the Christian tradition paradoxically becomes the global focus for the display of its deep and pervasive doctrinal schisms.

There is a further dimension to the manner in which shrines and their sacred powers are perceived, one that has to do with what one might call their temporal status. Pilgrimage shrines differ in their perceived relation to historical time. Stirrat, in an earlier publication (1984), identifies two modalities of the sacred, which respectively incorporate different notions of time. One modality he labels the 'Eliadean' sacred, timeless and ahistorical; the other is a 'Durkheimian' sacred, anchored in society and history. There is a hierarchical tension between the two, with the eternal and timeless being presented as superior to the time-bound world of finite existence. At super-shrines like the Hindu centre of Benares, Stirrat claims, religious activity embraces both worlds, with no distinction drawn between the pragmatic and the transcendent: 'religious activities at such shrines are both matters for making merit for the eternal life and means of gaining benefits in this world' (1984: 208).

In the Christian tradition, this continuing mediation between timeless and time-bound sacredness is effected largely through charismatic or visionary individuals such as Padre Pio, Brother Lambert, Bishop Aponsu, and St Bernadette. During their lifetimes, as long as their religious activities are enmeshed with political and economic changes and processes, such cult heroes and heroines are viewed by the official church with profound ambivalence. As already mentioned, it is only when such a person dies that the church is able to assert its full authority over the shrine he or she has bequeathed. There commonly ensues a process whereby the clergy will attempt to shift the cultic focus from this-worldly to other-worldly preoccupations: in other words, to transmute the legacy of the holy person from a time-bound, Durkheimian sacredness into a timeless, Eliadean one.

In some instances, such a wholesale shift is resisted by devotees, as at Lourdes, where the pragmatic miracle discourse of the pilgrims confronts the transcendent, sacrificial discourse of officialdom. In others, however, it is enthusiastically embraced. According to McKevitt, the devotees of Padre Pio, for example,

> attempt to live permanently, not in the historical time and space of the Sangiovannesi, but in the ritual time and space of the pilgrim. This they can only do by remaining as much as possible in the vicinity of the shrine, by eschewing the company of the Sangiovannesi and other non-devotees of Pio, and living lives that are clearly not social in the normal, moral sense.[7]

Clearly, the ideal – like Turner's goal of communitas – is impossible to achieve, but the resident devotees pursue it as far as the exigencies of life permit. In so doing, they earn the fulsome contempt and loathing of the local townspeople. For the latter, Pio's work and legacy are located squarely within the historical domain. His greatest miracle was the building of the hospital, the Casa Sollievo della Sofferenza, and stimulating the development of the town – although, as we have seen, the townspeople feel they have been excluded from many of the benefits of these material blessings.

What all this demonstrates is that it is the meanings and ideas which officials, pilgrims, and locals invest in the shrine – meanings and ideas which are determinately shaped by their political and religious, national and regional, ethnic and class backgrounds – which help to give the shrine its religious capital, though this investment might well be in a variety of theological currencies. The power of a shrine, therefore, derives in large part from its character almost as a religious void, a ritual space capable of accommodating diverse meanings and practices – though of course the shrine staff might attempt, with varying degrees of success, to impose a single, official discourse. This, in the final analysis, is what confers upon a major shrine its essential, universalistic character: its capacity to absorb and reflect a multiplicity of religious discourses, to be able to offer a variety of clients what each of them desires. Universalism is ultimately constituted not by a unification of discourses but rather by the capacity of a cult to entertain and respond to a plurality. The sacred centre, then, in this perspective, appears as a vessel into which pilgrims devoutly pour their hopes, prayers, and aspirations. And in a perfect illustration of the classic Marxist model of fetishization and alienation, the shrine then appears to its devotees as if it were itself dispensing the divine power and healing balm which they seek.

THE SUFFERING BODY IN PILGRIMAGE DISCOURSE

The counter-example of Jerusalem notwithstanding, it is this thaumaturgic power of healing upon which the renown of the vast majority of pilgrimage shrines rests. It is somewhat surprising, then, that attention has been focused hitherto mainly on priests and healthy pilgrims; the role of sick pilgrims and lay helpers at pilgrimage shrines has not been examined in any great detail. Skultans (1987a, 1987b) has recently discussed the ways in which female pilgrims try to effect miraculous cures for their mentally handicapped and disturbed relatives through trance and spirit possession at a Hindu shrine in the Indian state of Maharashtra, while Sallnow (1987) touches on the healing aspects of the shrine of Señor de Wank'a in Peru. But the involvement of lay organizers in the handling of sick pilgrims, and indeed the significance of sick persons at pilgrimage shrines, has been virtually ignored.

The first two chapters in this book, therefore, lead us into territory previously unexplored. The shrine which Dahlberg and Eade investigate – Lourdes – provides a wealth of material for a study of the role of sick pilgrims and their lay helpers. Although the shrine was intimately associated with the development of official church teaching concerning the Immaculate Conception of Christ's mother,[8] its popular attraction was bound up with the reports of miraculous cures involving the spring uncovered by Bernadette during one of her visions. Sick pilgrims featured at a very early stage in organized pilgrimage to Lourdes, and the French National pilgrimage sponsored some particularly spectacular rituals in the late nineteenth and early twentieth centuries, in which the sick were urged to get up and walk. Although considerable changes have taken place since, the suffering bodies of the sick pilgrims play a central role in the journeys of groups to and from Lourdes and at the shrine itself.

The significance of the suffering body varies according to the structure of the pilgrim group. For 'healthy' pilgrims in the Liverpool diocesan pilgrimage and the Handicapped Children's Trust pilgrimage, described by Dahlberg, sick pilgrims served to unite a group of near strangers into a coherent single group, both through the physical care of the sick by lay helpers and through the construction of supernatural discourses around the meaning and value of the suffering body. The journey to the shrine brought the sick from the margins of secular society to the centre of a temporary community travelling towards the sacred. On arrival, the sick pilgrims found themselves the focus of attention in the public places and rituals, where human physical imperfection was placed in an exalted position.

The physical body and its imperfections thereby become the focus for meanings which constitute the pilgrims as a social body – a transient community of sick and healthy travellers. In the third example cited by Dahlberg – a commercially organized pilgrimage – the sick were absent as a category organizing the group at the level of practice, but were nevertheless present for the group as a category at the level of consciousness. For one member of this group, the concept of healing was widened to embrace not just curing sickness but the eradication of all forms of imperfection.

The physical suffering of sick pilgrims was interpreted in diverse ways according to the structures of the various pilgrim groups and the social positions of individual pilgrims. However, the meanings attached to 'sickness' can be incorporated within the two contrasting discourses mentioned earlier. The miracle discourse directs attention to the possibility of a dramatic healing of physical infirmity. The sacrificial discourse, on the other hand, refines and sanctifies physical suffering, and by extension all forms of suffering, by focusing on the redemptive sacrifice of Jesus Christ through the crucifixion. These ideological differences are finally located within what Dahlberg sees as a Roman Catholic tradition concerning incarnation and the relationship between body and soul.

Dahlberg's data and analysis encourage a widening of the perspective on pilgrimage in western Europe, and suggest possibilities for future research on other Roman Catholic shrines throughout the world where miraculous cures have been reported. At the same time, the specificity of each shrine must be borne in mind. Lourdes does appear to be exceptional with regard to the large numbers of sick pilgrims who come on organized pilgrimages to the shrine. The processing of the infirm, moreover, is effected by a hierarchy of lay helpers which appears to be far more elaborate and cosmopolitan than at other Catholic shrines. The other healing shrines discussed in this volume – San Giovanni Rotondo in Italy and shrines in Sri Lanka and the Andes – have no comparable organizational structures.

Accordingly, at Lourdes, a substantial proportion of visitors are both pilgrims and, as lay helpers, controllers of the activities of their fellow pilgrims once they have arrived at the shrine. Eade's chapter, focused on the Hospitality of Our Lady of Lourdes, describes the tensions and conflicts which ensue. The Hospitallers are responsible for directing the movement of pilgrims at particular locales within the religious precincts of the shrine. They handle the bodies of the sick pilgrims and help both the sick and the healthy to bathe in waters which are popularly associated with miraculous healing. They also have considerable influence outside the baths, on the esplanade where miraculous cures have been recorded during the Blessed Sacrament procession. Yet despite the regimentation which the Hospitallers are obliged to impose, enterprising pilgrims find numerous ways to circumvent their power and to shape proceedings according to their own wishes.

The focus of Eade's analysis, then, is the power of the lay helpers and the ability of pilgrims to resist that power in the context of practices concerning the body. His discussion complements Dahlberg's in examining further the manifold practices associated with the miracle and sacrificial discourses. Hospitallers are required by their superiors and the religious organizers of the shrine to play down the miraculous in favour of an interpretation which emphasizes the healing role of the church's sacraments and the redemptive sacrifice of Our Lady's son, Jesus Christ. However, the implementation of official policy is limited by the investment of many of the pilgrims, and also of the Hospitallers themselves, in the miracle discourse. The Hospitality organization lacks the systematic integration of levels and practices which would ensure uniformity within its ranks. Moreover, the sick can to a degree insist on following their own practices, especially when it comes to bathing in the waters of the miraculous spring.

The implementation of an official interpretation through specific practices, therefore, is compromised by the lack of integration between practices and by the pilgrims' pursuit of their own strategies. At the same time, the pilgrims' freedom to do what they like and go where they please is also constrained by the procedures developed by the Hospitality and other organizers at the shrine. Tension and conflict are integral to this interplay of diverse practices, as large numbers of pilgrims move around and through the various sacred locales of the domaine.

Eade's account provides further illustration of the complex relationships between power and resistance, control and freedom of choice, hierarchy and equality evident at other Catholic shrines. The two chapters on Lourdes, however, underscore the importance of examining the particularities of a shrine's emergence and development as well as of measuring its similarities with other shrines elsewhere. The history of Lourdes has been shaped by specific conflicts within France between church and state, and by its intimate links with the papacy. In the nineteenth century, belief in miraculous healing was actively promoted by the church hierarchy in order to refute secular rationalism, while the visions of Bernadette Soubirous, confirming as they did the recently promulgated doctrine of the Immaculate Conception of Mary, provided the church with a timely opportunity to convince the faithful of papal authority and infallibility. Today, official emphasis has switched from the miracle to the sacrificial discourse, and organizations such as the Hospitality of lay helpers offer the shrine's clerical controllers a useful, if only partially effective, instrument in encouraging this change in orientation amongst the pilgrims. These ideological shifts revolve ultimately around the central and inextricably entwined symbols of the sick body and the possibilities for cure, and the sin-stained soul and the possibilities for redemption.

McKevitt's chapter on San Giovanni Rotondo reveals other facets of body symbolism in the context of pilgrimage. While Dahlberg and Eade concentrate on visiting pilgrims, McKevitt, as we have seen, is principally concerned with the perspective of the local townspeople on the shrine of Padre Pio. As already mentioned, the Sangiovannesi and the devotees of Pio do not share the same estimation of the saint's significance. While devotees are motivated by the meaning of Pio's suffering for their own spiritual and physical welfare, the Sangiovannesi emphasize the Capuchin's material legacy to the region, in particular the hospital for whose construction he was responsible.

This conjunction of a sophisticated modern hospital and the healing shrine of a suffering stigmatist aptly symbolizes the variety of contrasting discourses operative in the cult. For the devotees, typically regarded as hysterical and disturbed by the locals, Pio's tomb is the point of entry into a sacred world, marked out as the place of his 'living crucifixion'. As such it is viewed primarily in terms of a sacrificial discourse, as a place of spiritual redemption, although of course miraculous healing powers are attributed to it as well. The hospital provides medical reinforcement to these thaumaturgic powers, such that the 'miracle' and 'medical' discourses concerning disease and cure are here closely intertwined. The local townspeople, by contrast, choose to emphasize what they see as the 'economic miracle' wrought by Padre Pio – how he revitalized a depressed corner of the Gargano and promoted the social and physical well-being of the community. They tend to operate, therefore, with a fourth type of discourse, a secular, socio-economic one, which downplays the spiritual and miraculous dimensions of the cult and which stresses what Pio did for them in life rather than what he is claimed to do for the 'foreign' pilgrims in death.

McKevitt's focus on the attitudes of the local residents to a shrine and its devotees could be fruitfully applied elsewhere. For example, despite the growth of Lourdes from a small village into a substantial town with one of the largest hotel complexes in France, the numerous descriptions of the shrine have paid scant attention to the townspeople whose livelihoods depend directly upon the annual influx of so many pilgrims. One might well encounter similarities here with San Giovanni Rotondo, with the Lourdais placing far less significance upon the healing of the body or spiritual redemption, and instead understanding the 'miracle of Lourdes' primarily in terms of improved living standards and increased economic opportunities.

Another issue which these chapters raise in relation to discourses about the body and its ailments, and which we suggest as a topic for further research, is the involvement of the professional medical services in the organization of healing shrines. At both Lourdes and San Giovanni Rotondo, doctors clearly play an important role. The investment of these professionals in the miracle and sacrificial discourses would need to be analysed in the context of current medical discourses about healing, and in terms of their positions within a profession where there may be considerable hostility to the notion of a miraculous cure (see Turner 1984). One would also need to explore the relationship between the doctors and the clergy, since both claim in different ways to be concerned with the welfare of the body. At Lourdes, for example, doctors have an institutionalized adversary role: alleged miracles are tested by pitting a medical discourse against the miracle discourse, such that scientific rationality is paradoxically deployed to prove the intervention of the divine.

Miraculous healing in the baths at Lourdes or at Padre Pio's shrine, of course, circumvents entirely the intermediary roles of both priest and doctor. The sacrificial discourse, on the other hand, allows for human intervention in dealing with suffering, through the provision either of a satisfying theodicy by priests or of medical treatment by doctors. Padre Pio's wish that the Casa Sollievo would lead to the emergence of a hospital city, where Christian doctors would further develop medical research, raises interesting questions about the relationship between doctors and priests, between medical and clerical institutions, and between discourses and practices concerning the body, all of which would need to be examined within the specific contexts of particular shrines.

The tensions and contradictions between miracle and sacrificial discourses are also evident at pilgrimage shrines beyond the European heartland. Sallnow's discussion of the Andean shrine of Señor de Wank'a in southern Peru shows how pilgrims and priests project quite different, yet overlapping, understandings of the significance of the shrine. The bodily symbolism of the iconography itself is inescapable: the shrine consists of an image, painted on a rock, of Christ undergoing flagellation prior to his crucifixion, and allegedly has its origins in a series of visions at the spot by a fugitive Indian in the seventeenth century. But the shrine is not just about suffering inflicted; it is also about suffering relieved. Its mytho-history contains a sequence in which a wealthy mine-owner was miraculously cured by the same personage, the Christ of Wank'a. For pilgrims today, these two aspects of the shrine are closely interconnected. Healthy devotees flagellate themselves and press crowns of thorns on their heads in imitation of Christ, while sick pilgrims come in the hope of a cure, perhaps being permitted to touch the miraculous rock itself, or otherwise simply bathing in the healing waters of the spring alongside the sanctuary.

This dialectic between bodily suffering voluntarily inflicted or endured and bodily suffering miraculously relieved and cured is a feature of pilgrimage in many religious traditions. At the Sri Lankan shrine of Kataragama, for example, devotees engage in spectacular acts of self-mortification, such as walking on live coals and suspending themselves on meat-hooks through the skin, in fulfilment of a vow to the shrine deity to repay a divine favour (see for example Obeyesekere 1978). Healthy pilgrims torture themselves in varying degrees in order to make themselves akin to their sick comrades, while the sick attend in the hope of becoming healthy.

In the Catholic tradition, pilgrimage has always been seen as a form of penance, and indeed was imposed as a punishment for secular offences in the Middle Ages (Sumption 1975). The hardships and dangers of the journey and the bodily privations which pilgrims were obliged to undergo were thought to win the penitential pilgrim God's forgiveness and grace. Yet while a similar orientation towards a sacrificial discourse cannot be discounted among the modern-day flagellants at Señor de Wank'a, their dominant motives tend to be material rather than spiritual. By voluntarily undergoing pain, the devotee hopes that his or her request for a material favour, for the devotee personally or for one of his or her family, will be granted by the shrine divinity. In this sense, the self-inflicted suffering is of a piece with the miracle discourse, for it is primarily geared towards prompting thaumaturgic intervention in the affairs of the living here and now, rather than towards gaining grace and spiritual redemption in the hereafter.

In the Christian tradition, however, the dialectic between bodily suffering and bodily restoration possesses a theological significance which goes far beyond a mere transactional exchange of human penance for divine favour. The doctrine of the physical resurrection of the unblemished body on the Day of Judgment, which early Christianity inherited from Judaism and which is maintained today by both the Roman Catholic and Orthodox churches, has always had the effect of blurring the distinction between the spiritual and the material domains, between the soul and the body. In terms of this doctrine, bodily imperfections and illnesses pass from being mere metaphors of original or committed sins to being the outward signs of the spiritual state of the soul: in this life, the human body is inevitably imperfect, but the risen corpse on the Last Day will be flawless and hence fit for the company of its creator.[9]

This eschatological transformation of the body was foreshadowed, in a highly telescoped fashion, by Christ's death, resurrection, and ascension to heaven. His tortured and broken body, however, bore not his own sins but those of all mankind.[10] Since then, numerous saints and would-be saints have been held to have emulated this process of anticipatory restoration and redemption, their frail or suffering bodies in life allegedly remaining incorrupt after their deaths, in readiness for their resurrection on the Last Day. Their spiritual redemption, in other words, is assured, and the sign of that assurance is a body that defies physical decay. The putatively incorrupt corpse of Bernadette Soubirous, the Lourdes visionary, lies on display in the church at Nevers, while those promoting the 'cause' of Padre Pio – that is, his official elevation to sainthood – are convinced that, when his tomb is eventually opened, his stigmatized body will show no signs of decay, thereby confirming absolutely his saintly status.

Given this tight nexus between spiritual salvation and corporeal wholeness in Christian belief, self-inflicted suffering and divine healing in the context of pilgrimage cults come to possess a sacred significance which is absent or less pronounced in other religious traditions. In the Catholic tradition at least, self-flagellation and other forms of voluntary torture serve to bring the physical body to a state of suffering and pain to match the sinful and anguished state of the soul. Miraculous healing, meanwhile, is intimately bound up with the forgiveness of sin and the receipt of grace, and serves as a kind of foretaste of the fate of the body on the Last Day.

Sin and suffering, grace and health are so closely interconnected that a pilgrimage comes to resemble an eschatological drama, with the terrible events of the Day of Judgment being played out in miniature. It is hardly surprising in this context that going on a pilgrimage is so often phrased in terms of death and rebirth.

Nevertheless, the attitudes of the Mercedarian priests at the shrine of Señor de Wank'a towards miraculous healing and physical penance are deeply ambivalent. On the one hand, they do not discourage either the emulation of Christ's Passion through such practices as flagellation or the notion of miraculous cures wrought by the shrine. On the other hand, they make no mention whatsoever of these 'popular' beliefs and practices in their sermons and homilies to the devotees. Here, the emphasis is wholly on the redemptive power of Christ, and on the moral example Christ set for family life. The official output, therefore, is phrased entirely within a sacrificial discourse, though it is clearly the investment of the majority of devotees in a miracle discourse which maintains the enormous inter-national popularity of the shrine.

The new generation of shrines in Sri Lanka offers yet another perspec-tive on bodily healing in the context of pilgrimage. Physical ailments and other misfortunes among Roman Catholics in Sri Lanka, Stirrat claims, are closely related to the declining social status and reduced political influence of the Catholic minority since independence. The corporate institution of the Roman Catholic Church can no longer provide adequate support for its members in a society where they are heavily outnumbered by Tamil Hindus and Sinhala Buddhists. Personal distress is explained increasingly in terms of a belief in sorcery, which the Buddhists also share. Sri Lankan Catholics, however, maintain an ideological distance from the majority community by enlisting the aid of powerful, charismatic individ-uals such as Brother Lambert, Norbert, and the self-styled Bishop Aponsu, who utilize trance and spirit possession to enable pilgrims to engage the supernatural powers of particular saints in their struggle with personal misfortune.

The clergy denounce such ritual practices as superstition and magic, but they have limited powers to prevent them as the shrines operate largely outside clerical control. Meanwhile, at the older shrines, the priests are attempting to advance a 'modern', sacrificial interpretation of pilgrimage and thereby to bring them into a Eurocentric tradition of Catholicism. Yet, at the same time, recourse even to these long-established shrines is being devalued by a church hierarchy which displays considerable ambivalence towards the very practice of pilgrimage. Claims of miraculous healing at these controlled shrines are denied, and Catholics are encouraged to adopt other forms of devotional activity. While in Europe reforms undertaken through the central authority of the church are creating tensions at shrines such as Lourdes between official and non-official discourses concerning suffering and cure, in Sri Lanka Catholics disaffected by such reforms can find comfort in the new wave of shrines where the miraculous healing of the body is promoted and celebrated, via practices which the official church disdains.[11]

SYMBOLIC EXCHANGE IN PILGRIMAGE

We have already referred on several occasions to the overtly transactional ethic of contemporary pilgrimage. In most cases, the dominant motive for going on a pilgrimage is to request some favour of God or the shrine divinity in return for simply having made the journey or for engaging in ancillary devotional exercises. As transformation stations between the earthly and heavenly realms, pilgrimage shrines are the pre-eminent centres for dealings between human beings and the divine. In many ways, they represent the stock exchanges of the religious economy. Using the shrine divinity as a mediator, physical suffering and penance are exchanged for material and spiritual favours, contracts are forged with the saints, sin is amortized by means of a tariff of devotional or ascetic practices, and in many instances indulgences[12] may be earned merely by dint of having attended the shrine festival and having expended earthly time in so doing.

Pilgrimage cults in the Christian tradition are pervaded by such manifold self-interested exchanges between humans and the divine, for their focal shrines are the principal repositories and dispensaries of grace and blessings in all their various material and non-material forms. Money is by no means excluded from these sacred exchanges. Indulgences may no longer be commuted and sold, but cash donations to the shrine custodians, purchases of candles, alms to beggars, indeed all kinds of monetary offerings can be fully incorporated into the religious marketing circuits of the shrine.

This market ideology embraces both the miracle and the sacrificial discourses. The two are distinguished only by the nature of the favours which it is hoped will be granted – material favours in this life or spiritual redemption in the next. Yet the emphasis on reciprocated giving and self-interest does contrast with a putative theme in Christian teaching concerning the free, 'pure' gift. The epitome of such a gift is held to be the sacrifice of Christ himself on behalf of all mankind, and the faithful are encouraged to follow his example. Pilgrimage provides them with an ideal opportunity to enter into the life of Christ, through supposedly following directly in his footsteps, as in the Holy Land, or by emulating his sufferings, as at Señor de Wank'a, or by simply demonstrating a fundamental Christian charity towards other pilgrims. Thus, at Lourdes, lay helpers are enjoined to set an example in self-sacrifice to other pilgrims by giving freely of their time and labour, and pilgrims who wish to pay the helpers in the baths for their assistance are reminded of the symbolic meaning of the free gift.

Now according to Parry (1986), the ideology of the pure gift and self-sacrifice is intimately related to the ideology of the reciprocated gift and self-interest. The Christian world, he argues, has seen the simultaneous development of 'a *universalistic* conception of purely disinterested giving' alongside the emergence of the notion of 'pure utility' (1986: 468). It is appropriate that pilgrimage shrines, given their interstitial status both in and out of time, and as both universalistic and place-bound, should play host in their devotional postures and practices to both ideologies.

For a strongly salvatory religion such as Catholicism, however, it is questionable whether the notion of purely disinterested giving can be anything other than a fiction. A person performing an ostensibly selfless act of charity or abnegation, while spurning the idea of tangible, earthly rewards, will automatically reap spiritual dividends, whether or not such was his or her intention. The issue of motive, therefore, becomes somewhat academic. A perceptive contemporary observer described Henry II's visit to Canterbury in July 1174 as an *imitatio Christi*, for, like Christ, he allowed himself to be beaten with scourges; 'save that Christ did this for the remission of our sins whereas Henry did it for the remission of his own' (quoted in Sumption 1975: 93). In whatever coin a devotee chooses to make his or her offerings – spiritual exercises, bodily privations or pecuniary deprivations – they all redound ultimately to his or her credit, either materially or spiritually. While the clergy might inveigh against the this-worldly attitude of pilgrims desirous of immediate material favours, their stress on the redemptive rather than on the miraculous power of the shrine amounts merely to a redirection of the transactional ethic, not to its rejection.

Mirroring the intensive sacred commerce mediated by a pilgrimage shrine, one frequently encounters equally intensive secular commerce taking place in or around the sanctuary precincts. The conjunction of markets and pilgrimage is well documented for many parts of the world. In the Cusco region of the central Andes, for example, the annual round of fairs and festivals of miraculous shrines is closely related to the ecology of the area and to the cycles of agricultural and pastoral production, marketing and consumption (Sallnow 1987). In the Old World, super-shrines such as Lourdes, Fatima, and the Holy Land have developed more permanent economic infrastructures for dealing with the continual influx of pilgrims, with hotels, banks, restaurants, shopping centres, and car parks established to cater for their temporal needs. Distasteful as such commercialism might appear to some devotees and to the shrine clergy – for many years, the Mercedarian priests at Señor de Wank'a fought the attempts of traders to establish a market outside the sanctuary – it is nevertheless of a piece with the religious dealings taking place within the cult itself. Ironically, it is very often the petty traders of shrine souvenirs – statuettes, spring water, guide books, devotional pictures, and so forth – who tend to attract the ire of the shrine staff, perhaps because they threaten most conspicuously the fragile boundary between religious devotion and workaday commerce, and by extension between the sacred and secular realms, which they are obliged to maintain.

CONCLUSION

Despite the pioneering work of the past two decades, the anthropological study of pilgrimage, and in particular of Christian pilgrimage, is still in its infancy. Ethnographically, the coverage is sparse. Within western Europe, we lack detailed anthropological studies even of such important shrines as Fatima in Portugal and Santiago de Compostela in Spain, as well as of local shrine networks such as those embraced by the *pardons* of Brittany or the *romerías* of Andalucia. In eastern Europe, where dramatic political and economic changes are currently proceeding apace, new cults such as that of the Virgin of Medjugorje in Yugoslavia or newly refurbished ones such as that of the Virgin of Czestochowa in Poland offer rich opportunities for the investigation of emergent state-centred and ethnic nationalisms.

Theoretically, too, there is enormous scope for advancement beyond the structuralist models that have tended to dominate the literature to date. The conflict and articulation between multiple discourses, the manifold differences in perceptions of a shrine and its powers both within and between denominations, and between pilgrims and staff, the significance of the suffering body in the context of healing shrines, the nature of the exchanges between human beings and the divine that give pilgrimage its central rationale – the themes which we have touched on in this introduction indicate just a few of the fruitful directions which pilgrimage research might take in the future. The contributions to this symposium, in their pursuit of these and other theoretical lines of enquiry, point the way forward.

NOTES

1 Bowman (1988), in a report on the conference, identified a persistent division between on the one hand the descriptive and phenomenological approaches of the historical and theological contributions, and on the other the more analytical and deconstructionist thrust of many of the anthropological and sociological papers.

2 For critiques of Durkheim's analysis of Australian Aboriginal ritual, see Stanner (1967) and Morton (1987).

3 Morinis (1984: 238–49) provides a comprehensive review of functionalist case-studies of pilgrimage.

4 It is worth noting in passing that Turner's ideas are echoed, though not acknowledged, in the work of a prominent French writer on Christian pilgrimage, Alphonse Dupront (1987). In his work, too, there is a generalizing thrust towards a universal model of pilgrimage, defined as a human quest for the sacred which generates a model of society based on fraternity and common well-being (1987: 414).

5 Literally 'mixed' race. In contemporary Peru it is used to connote 'an orientation towards Hispanic cultural mores, versus "indigena"', Indian culture. See Sallnow below, pp. 142–3.

6 Mercedarians: 'Popular name for the Order of Our Lady of Mercy, derived from the Spanish word *merced* (mercy).' New Catholic Encyclopædia (1967: 669). The Order was founded in 1218 'for the ransom of Christian slaves' at a ceremony in Barcelona cathedral attended by King James of Aragon (ibid: 670).

7 See McKevitt below, p.93.

8 The Immaculate Conception refers to Mary's unique exemption from the stain of original sin.

9 For a discussion of Orthodox theology on this point, see Danforth (1982).

10 Interestingly, Christ's body was not completely restored on his resurrection, for doubting Thomas was enjoined to inspect the nailmarks on Christ's hands and to put his own hand into the rupture made by a soldier's spear at the crucifixion (John 20: 27).

11 See, for example, Camus 1989; Favret-Saada 1980; Giovannini 1981.

12 An indulgence is remission on the time a soul must spend in purgatory before gaining admission to heaven. An indulgence may be partial – conventionally measured in days – or plenary, that is, total.

REFERENCES

Bowman, G. (1988) 'Pilgrimage conference report', *Anthropology Today* 4(6): 20–3.

Camus, D. (1989) *Pouvoirs Sorciers*, Paris: Éditions Imago.

Cohn, B. S. and Marriott, M. (1958) 'Networks and centres in the integration of Indian civilisation', *Journal of Social Research* 1: 1–9.

Durkheim, E. (1912) *The Elementary Forms of the Religious Life*, trans. J. W. Swain, London: Allen & Unwin, 1964.

Eickelman, D. (1976) *Moroccan Islam*, Austin: Texas University Press.

Eliade, M. (1963) 'Sacred places: temple, palace, "centre of the world"', in *Patterns in Comparative Religion*, New York: World Publishing Co.

Favret-Saada, J. (1980) *Deadly Words*, trans. C. Cullen, Cambridge: Cambridge University Press.

Fought, J. (1969) 'Chorti (Mayan) ceremonial organisation', *American Anthropologist* 71: 472–6.

Giovannini, M. J. (1981) 'Woman: a dominant symbol within the cultural system of a Sicilian town', *Man* 16: 408–26.

Gross, D. (1971) 'Ritual and conformity: a religious pilgrimage to northeastern Brazil', *Ethnology* 10: 129–48.

Marx, E. (1977) 'Communal and individual pilgrimage: the region of saints' tombs in South Sinai', in R. P. Werbner (ed.) *Regional Cults*, London: Academic Press.

Messerschmidt, D. A. and Sharma, J. (1981) 'Hindu pilgrimage in the Nepal Himalayas', *Current Anthropology* 22: 571–2.

Morinis, E. A. (1984) *Pilgrimage in the Hindu Tradition: A Case Study of West Bengal*, Delhi: Oxford University Press.

Morton, J. (1987) 'The effectiveness of totemism: "increase ritual" and resource control in central Australia', *Man* 22: 453–74.

New Catholic Encyclopædia (1967), 9: 669–70.

Obeyesekere, G. (1966) 'The Buddhist pantheon in Ceylon and its extensions', in M. Nash (ed.) *Anthropological Studies in Theravada Buddhism*, New Haven: Yale University Southeast Asian Studies.

———— (1978) 'The fire walkers of Kataragama: the rise of *bhakti* religiosity in Buddhist Sri Lanka', *Journal of Asian Studies* 37: 353–70.

Parry, J.P. (1986) '*The gift*, the Indian gift and the "Indian gift"', *Man* 21: 453–73.

Pfaffenberger, B. (1979) 'The Kataragama pilgrimage: Hindu–Buddhist interaction and its significance in Sri Lanka's polyethnic social system', *Journal of Asian Studies* 38: 253–70.

Rabinow, P. (1975) *Symbolic Domination: Cultural Form and Historical Change in Morocco*, Chicago: University of Chicago Press.

Redfield, R. (1956) *Peasant Society and Culture: An Anthropological Approach to Civilization*, Chicago: University of Chicago Press.

Sallnow, M. J. (1981) 'Communitas reconsidered: the sociology of Andean pilgrimage', *Man* 16: 163–82.

———— (1987) *Pilgrims of the Andes: Regional Cults in Cusco*, Washington, DC: Smithsonian Institution Press.

Skultans, V. (1987a) 'Trance and the management of mental illness among Maharashtrian families', *Anthropology Today* 3(1): 2–4.

_____ (1987b) 'The management of mental illness among Maharashtrian families: a case-study of a Mahanubhav healing temple', *Man* 22: 661–79.

Spiro, M. (1970) *Buddhism and Society: A Great Tradition and its Burmese Vicissitudes*, New York: Harper & Row.

Srinivas, M.N. (1967) 'The cohesive role of Sanskritization', in P. Mason (ed.) *India and Ceylon: Unity and Diversity*, London: Oxford University Press.

Stanner, W. E. H. (1967) 'Reflections on Durkheim and Aboriginal religion', in M. Freedman (ed.) *Social Organization: Essays Presented to Raymond Firth*, London: Frank Cass.

Stirrat, R. L. (1984) 'Catholics and the riots in historical perspective', in J. Manor (ed.) *Sri Lanka in Change and Crisis*, London: Croom Helm.

Sumption, J. (1975) *Pilgrimage: An Image of Medieaval Religion*, London: Faber & Faber.

Turner, B. S. (1984) *The Body and Society: Explorations in Social Theory*, Oxford: Basil Blackwell.

Turner, V. W. (1974a) 'Pilgrimages as social processes', in *Dramas, Fields and Metaphors: Symbolic Action in Human Society*, Ithaca: Cornell University Press.

_____ (1974b) 'Pilgrimage and communitas', *Studia Missionalia* 23: 305–27.

Turner, V. W. and Turner, E. (1978) *Image and Pilgrimage in Christian Culture: Anthropological Perspectives*, Oxford: Basil Blackwell.

Van der Veer, P. (1984) 'Structure and anti-structure in Hindu pilgrimage to Ayodhya', in K. Ballhatchet and D. Taylor (eds) *Changing South Asia: Religion and Society*, Hong Kong and London: Asian Research Service for the Centre of South Asian Studies, School of Oriental and African Studies, University of London.

Werbner, R. P. (1977) 'Introduction', in R. P. Werbner (ed.) *Regional Cults*, London: Academic Press.

Wolf, E. (1958) 'The Virgin of Guadalupe: a Mexican national symbol', *Journal of American Folklore* 71(1): 34–9.

Chapter one

The body as a principle of holism
Three pilgrimages to Lourdes

Andrea Dahlberg

INTRODUCTION

This chapter gives an account of three contemporary English Catholic pilgrimages to Lourdes. The ethnography describes the way in which the suffering body is taken from the margins of secular society and becomes the means of uniting temporary groups of strangers making the pilgrimage. This process is elaborated and intensified at the shrine itself: through the rites and symbolism of the cult, the sick pilgrim comes to assume a symbolic identity of supernatural significance. It is suggested that this central role of the suffering body in these pilgrimages has significance for our understanding of Catholicism more generally. This is demonstrated by a consideration of the implicit place and implicit meaning of the body in Catholicism, and of how this contrasts at various points with the symbolism of the body in certain Protestant traditions.

The ethnography is taken from a four-year study of English Catholics at Lourdes. Four months were spent at the shrine itself, while approximately twelve months were spent making journeys with pilgrims and tourists. Many of these people were also visited and interviewed in their homes, both before and after the journey. A full account of the study is given in Dahlberg (1987).

THE HISTORY OF THE SHRINE AT LOURDES

Strictly speaking, the shrine at Lourdes has its origins in a series of eighteen apparitions of the Virgin Mary to a 14-year-old girl of the town during the year 1858. The only academic historian to have produced a major study of Lourdes in its nineteenth-century context, the American Thomas Kselman, describes how the young visionary was encouraged by the local parish priest and how the bishop too took up her cause with enthusiasm. Nothing in her reports of her visions, or in her own life, opposed any teachings of the church actively propagated at the time; on the contrary, both the visions and the miraculous cures reportedly following her visions were exemplary types of the means used by an embattled nineteenth-century French church to fight back against the political, scientific, and social forces which were weakening its temporal power.

Kselman (1978) shows how education and family law during this period assisted the state in its attempt to wrest power from the church. He describes the corrosive effect of science upon forms of religious explanation and how the social forces of industrialization and urbanization further reduced the church's temporal power. He argues that the church used miracles and prophecies as part of a defensive strategy to reassert and defend itself, claiming that 'in the nineteenth century, the church made a substantial effort to develop regional and national miracle cults. This institutional initiative was accompanied by an expansion of the miraculous to include literate and middle-class Catholics' (Kselman 1978: 59).[1]

The church thus deployed miracle cults such as that of Lourdes to defend itself against the attacks of rationalist philosophers of the Enlightenment tradition, asserting that knowledge obtained through supernatural means was superior to knowledge constructed from reason. This superior, mystical knowledge was associated with 'simple' people and not with the educated. The visionary of Lourdes was a good example. She was young, she came from a very poor family which had been reduced to living in an abandoned jail-cell during the time of her apparitions, she was slow to learn, and there are numerous stories describing her failure to grasp even the simplest elements of religious instruction. She also suffered ill-health. She was thus socially, intellectually, and physically disadvantaged. Yet, as the church of the time asserted so strongly, it was to her that the Mother of God chose to appear, and it was her visions which revealed a miraculous spring curative of conditions and diseases which had failed to respond to medical treatment.

The French church of this time valued these miraculous cures chiefly for their apologetic value. The assertion of the superiority of mystical over rational knowledge was elaborately demonstrated at Lourdes. Where Catholic shrines traditionally kept records of miracles reported by pilgrims, the French church developed this practice into a means of investigating miraculous cures, with the intention of providing medical proof of their existence. The miracles of healing were investigated by doctors, who hoped to produce evidence to refute their rationalist opponents. The rationalists claimed that any cures at the shrine were in fact produced by the mineral content of the water, hysteria, delusion, or straightforward fabrication.

However, it was not only the French church (or more specifically, the hierarchy) which took up and promoted the cult of Lourdes as a defensive strategy. The pope – Pius IX – displayed an almost immediate interest in the apparitions, and subsequently used them to justify two of the most controversial dogmas of modern times.

Pius IX became pope in 1846. He began his pontificate by declaring an amnesty for political prisoners and exiles, and by supporting the cause of Italian unification. In 1848, however, he refused to lend his armies to help the northern Italian insurgents against the Austrians, and when the revolutionaries seized Rome they drove him out. The following year, the French took Rome and allowed him to return to the city. These events marked a turning point in his rule: he abandoned his former liberalism and began to assert the power of the church by affirming it as the exclusive representative of supernatural power. It was during this period that he saw his temporal power decrease markedly. Between the years 1860 and 1870 he lost all the papal states, and was left only with the city of Rome; this, too, was taken from him in 1870 by Victor Emmanuel's troops. The following year the Law of Guarantees was instituted, which declared the pope's territories forfeit to the Italian state and which robbed him of virtually all temporal power. Refusing to acknowledge himself as a subject of the new kingdom, he chose to remain isolated within the Vatican, never to cross its borders again; he became a self-imposed prisoner in his last remaining territory.

Pius IX reacted to the loss of his temporal power by a vigorous repudiation of liberalism, socialism, rationalism, and pantheism – most famously and forcibly in the Syllabus of Errors of 1864. Historians and theologians today sometimes refer to the 'syllabus mentality' of Pius IX, meaning a closed, combative mind. On the other hand, he asserted the supernatural basis of the church and of his own power through two dogmas – the dogma of the Immaculate Conception of Mary (1854) and the dogma of the Infallibility of the Pope (1870). Both these dogmas were justified with reference to the Marian apparitions at Lourdes.

The Blessed Virgin Mary said rather little to the visionary Bernadette Soubirous at Lourdes in 1858. One of the things she did say, however, was, 'I am the Immaculate Conception'. The bishops and the pope interpreted this rather cryptic phrase as support for the dogma enunciated four years earlier, which holds that Mary was exempt from original sin from the moment of her conception. Although this had been a popular folk

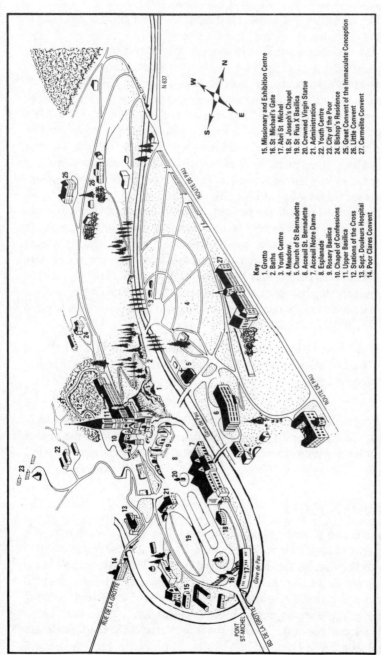

Key
1. Grotto
2. Baths
3. Youth Centre
4. Meadow
5. Church of St Bernadette
6. Acceuil St. Bernadette
7. Acceuil Notre Dame
8. Esplanade
9. Rosary Basilica
10. Upper Basilica
11. Chapel of Confessions
12. Stations of the Cross
13. Sept. Douleurs Hospital
14. Poor Clares Convent
15. Missionary and Exhibition Centre
16. St Michael's Gate
17. Abri St Michel
18. St Joseph's Chapel
19. St Pius X Basilica
20. Crowned Virgin Statue
21. Administration
22. Youth Centre
23. City of the Poor
24. Bishop's Residence
25. Great Convent of the Immaculate Conception
26. Little Convent
27. Carmelite Convent

Figure 1.1 Map of Lourdes: the domaine

belief since medieval times, it had until then never attained the status of dogma.

The Lourdes apparitions, however, were not only interpreted as confirming the dogma of the Immaculate Conception. They were also used to justify the power and ability of the pope to pronounce without error on matters of faith. During the controversy surrounding the passing of the dogma of the Infallibility of the Pope, it was claimed that the Virgin Mary appeared at Lourdes in order to support him. Successive popes repeated this claim; thus, Pius X declared in an encyclical letter of 1904 that 'Pius IX had hardly defined it to be of Catholic faith that Mary was from her origin exempt from sin, when the Virgin herself began performing miracles at Lourdes' (Carlen 1981 (III): 21).

Subsequent popes have similarly invoked the apparitions at Lourdes as a means of legitimating their power, and have thereby helped to promote the cult within the universal church. Pius X extended the mass of the Immaculate Conception, composed under the direction of Leo XIII, to the universal church. Pius XI canonized Bernadette. Pius XII described the relationship between the dogmas of the Immaculate Conception and the Infallibility of the Pope on the one hand and the apparitions at Lourdes on the other in the following words:

> The Blessed Virgin Mary herself wanted to confirm by some special sign the definition which the Vicar on earth of her Divine Son had pronounced.
>
> (Carlen 1981 (III): 21)

> [At] Lourdes, four years after the definition of the dogma, the Immaculate Virgin herself gave supernatural confirmation to the declaration of the Supreme Teacher, by appearance, conversations, and miracles.
>
> (Carlen 1981 (V): 29)

LOURDES TODAY

Over four million pilgrims and tourists visit Lourdes each year, the majority of them from western Europe. They visit the shrine most intensively in the period between Easter and October. This seasonal population is served by an immense number of shops, hotels, and cafés clustered around the shrine. These institutions employ around 4500 workers during the pilgrimage season, and most of them close during the winter months. The resident population of the town is only around 18,000 (Chaudefaud 1981; Rinschede 1986).

For the English Catholics described in this chapter, Lourdes is one of a series of shrines known and/or visited. A significant part of the identity of Lourdes was drawn from contrasting it with others in this series. Chief amongst these were Rome and the Holy Land. There is a saying, 'Rome is the head of the church but Lourdes is its heart'. This expresses the importance of the cult of Lourdes within the church in the eyes of its devotees, and also emphasizes the emotive nature of the cult. The force of the saying is derived from an implicit contrast between the urban maleness of Rome and the rural feminine nature of Lourdes; Rome is about leadership and authority, Lourdes is the 'emotional side of Catholicism'. Lourdes is renowned as a Marian healing shrine and as a place where the sick and all those subject to some form of bodily suffering go in search of help.

For the church today, Lourdes may be classed as an international evangelical centre. Kselman has demonstrated the early support of the bishops for the shrine at Lourdes and has shown how the propagation of the cult was due to a significant extent to their enthusiasm. Support from this same quarter can be seen today. Almost every bishop in the United Kingdom accompanies his diocese on an annual pilgrimage to Lourdes, and the same can be said for most parts of western Europe. The priests at Lourdes communicate directly with the spiritual directors of these pilgrimages, resulting in a high degree of similarity in pilgrimage organization. Interviews with priests on western European diocesan pilgrimages revealed that they saw the pilgrimage as a means of stimulating enthusiasm and devotion amongst the laity and that they sought to channel this enthusiasm into the church itself by encouraging pilgrims to attend weekly mass and other devotions on their return home. Many of these priests also travelled to Lourdes with pilgrimages organized by charities or commercial concerns; the authorities at Lourdes repeatedly request of the bishops that they provide priests to accompany all Lourdes pilgrimages from their dioceses.

This means that the Lourdes pilgrimage is structured into the life of most western European dioceses and this, in turn, has implications for the identity of the pilgrimage and for the type of pilgrim who is drawn to it. The pilgrims described here were practising Catholics who were in the main supportive of their church and its priesthood. The Lourdes pilgrimage is understood by them to be directly compatible with their experience of the church today; it was not, for instance, a significant forum for criticism of the reforms of Vatican II or for the church's stand on contemporary social or political issues. Thus one can still see an alliance of the 'great' and 'little' traditions of Catholicism as described by Kselman within the formally organized pilgrimages to Lourdes today.[1]

THE LIVERPOOL ARCHDIOCESAN PILGRIMAGE

With the exception of the war years, the archdiocese of Liverpool has had an annual pilgrimage to Lourdes since 1923.[2]

In July 1985, 1600 pilgrims from the diocese travelled to Lourdes by rail, coach, and aeroplane. The majority travelled together by rail with the archbishop and two of the three bishops of the archdiocese. One hundred and ten hospitalized sick pilgrims travelled together in the last carriage of the train, many of them arriving at the station on stretchers or in wheelchairs. This group of pilgrims were cared for during the 26-hour journey by male and female voluntary helpers known as *brancardiers* and handmaids. Few of these helpers had any medical training but they were responsible for the routine daily care of the sick. Doctors and nurses were available to provide specialist medical care where necessary. There were many more sick pilgrims scattered throughout the population of ordinary pilgrims. Some of these were children under 16 who were travelling with parents, others were well enough to care for themselves on a daily basis, and a third group were those who simply had not identified themselves as sick pilgrims to the organizers of the pilgrimage.

Most of the pilgrims were over 45, female, and travelling in small groups of four or five. A very high percentage had been before and many of the helpers had been five, ten, or even twenty or thirty times before. They said the Lourdes pilgrimage was 'addictive', 'you just get hooked and keep coming back'. A priest referred to one of his parishioners as 'a Lourdes groupie'. One woman had been making the pilgrimage every year since 1923 (with the exception of the war years) and one man said he now feels 'a part of Lourdes'.

The majority of the handmaids and *brancardiers* were unknown to the sick pilgrims before the journey. During the early stages of the journey, many of the sick pilgrims were apprehensive about what lay ahead. Some were uncomfortable in railway seats not made for invalids. Others were reticent about requesting help from the volunteers. Those who had not been to Lourdes before were divided in their attitude to the journey. Some had wanted to come for years, but, faced with the discomforts of travel, were wishing that they were back within the safe confines of the hospital or bedroom where familiar staff or kin attended to their needs. It was the

physical dependence of the sick upon the healthy which initially broke
down this reticence.

During the journey the sick were moved from the margins of secular
society to become the centre of a temporary community travelling towards
the sacred. This movement was accomplished primarily through a series
of reversals or inversions of their place and role in society. The sick
pilgrims found themselves in public places surrounded by strangers who
paid to work for them. In other words, the shrine is approached with
human physical imperfection in an exalted position.

While the journey bonded the sick pilgrims and the helpers together,
it was the series of daily activities at the shrine itself which extended this
process and constructed a larger symbolic identity for the sick. The hostel
at the shrine where the sick pilgrims stayed was a scene of constant
activity. *Brancardiers,* handmaids, nurses, and doctors were in attendance
serving meals and transporting the sick to and from daily services. Every
evening, members of the youth group entertained them with songs and
music. Many of the sick pilgrims visited bars and cafés and were sometimes seen dancing in the hospital courtyard at night. Conditions in the
hostel were well below those to which most of the sick pilgrims were
accustomed at home. The beds were crammed close together, there was
little privacy, and few of them were able to get enough sleep. The women's
ward appeared less like a hospital and more like a scene from a novel
about a midnight feast in a girls' boarding school: an atmosphere of chaos
and excitement reigned, overstuffed suitcases spilled out from under the
beds, sweets were passed around, and couples were huddled together in
intense whispered conversation.

The complaints of the sick pilgrims also revealed the dramatic inver-
sion of their place in secular society. They said there was 'no privacy' and
'no peace'. Each day, pilgrims staying in the hotels would come to the
hostel and volunteer to care for the sick. They were generally told that
there were sufficient helpers. In fact, many quarrels between the handmaids occurred because there were too many of them for the work
available. Ordinary pilgrims fought and competed to work for the sick.
The sick pilgrims were sometimes overwhelmed by the attention bestowed on them, but suppressed their dissatisfaction for fear of appearing
ungrateful. They followed the ordinary pilgrims in describing their discomforts as penances and in striving to live out an idealized set of social
relationships which they saw as essential to the experience of pilgrimage.

Why do these people come to Lourdes? And why do so many return
year after year? When I collected the 'Lourdes histories' of the pilgrims,

a pattern emerged. It was an experience of bereavement, the birth of a handicapped or retarded child, or an illness or tragedy which motivated the first pilgrimage and in many cases set up a pattern of repeated pilgrimage. This pattern was found amongst all categories of pilgrim: it was present amongst the handmaids and *brancardiers*, the 'healthy' pilgrims, and the sick pilgrims alike.

Pilgrims who sought a cure or amelioration for their suffering were constantly reminded of the superiority of the soul over the body as well as of the spiritual benefits conferred through bodily suffering. The pilgrimage priests convey this explicitly in sermons, while at the same time affirming the reality of miraculous healings at Lourdes. The voluntary helpers communicate this more subtly and perhaps more effectively by their exceptionally generous care of the sick. Their work speaks of the value of the sick pilgrim and of the value of sickness: the sick are treated as attractive people who are given the central place in the rituals at the shrine and draw the kind of attention reserved for celebrities in society generally. In this latter respect, the sick are not treated as individuals in the sense of being private citizens, nor are they treated as patients; at Lourdes each sick pilgrim has a kind of public identity like a celebrity or famous person. Strangers will approach sick pilgrims and speak to them, touch or stroke them, give them small gifts and request their prayers. All these actions affirm the value of physical disability.

This tension between desired miracles of healing and the sanctification of physical suffering was to be found throughout all the major services of the pilgrimage.[3] At the Mass of the Anointing of the Sick, for instance, it was said that the service aimed to give the sick 'the strength and grace to bear their illness'. The archbishop described the sick pilgrim as being closer to Christ than the other pilgrims, and it was said that the sick were honoured by this service because 'they make up all that has still to be undergone by Christ for the sake of his body the church'. This rite described sickness both as a sign of sin, and also as a means of participating in the Passion of Christ. As a sign of sin it is negatively valued and a miracle cure is implicitly valued, but as a means of participating in the Passion it is positively valued as leading to the eradication of sin. Given that this pilgrimage is organized by the priests of the archdiocese, it is significant that it was the church which was described as the recipient of this sacrificial act.

Each of these contradictory meanings of physical suffering can be linked to a divine figure. Christ in the Passion exemplifies the sanctification of suffering, but it is Mary as Our Lady of Lourdes who embodies the physical and moral perfection the pilgrims seek. They treated the grotto where the apparitions occurred as a place where Mary still resides, and they described praying there as speaking directly to Mary. Lourdes water was said to contain or transmit Marian healing power: it is the medium through which Mary communicates something of her perfection to the pilgrim.

The return journey was the scene of many critical discussions of the pilgrimage. A pilgrim from my hotel claimed that 'it wasn't as good as last year', but was surprised when I asked if he would return the following year – 'of course!' Other pilgrims who knew of my study of the pilgrimage sought me out to give me their critical assessment: 'The youth group should travel with the rest of us; they're set apart and made a fuss of, it makes two pilgrimages, not one.' Most of these discussions were about better ways of organizing the pilgrimage, whether or not the pilgrimage itself or certain of its activities were 'as good' as last year's or 'as good' as they should be, and whether or not the ideals of the pilgrims had been realized. The assessments about whether something was 'good' concerned the nature of the religious experience of the pilgrims: they expect an ecstatic religious experience centred on the sick. The ideals of the pilgrims are more concerned with their social relations: there should be no quarrelling or fighting, and everybody should work together in a spirit of cheerful co-operation. This, of course, is not what happens in practice, and pilgrims are more inclined to express dissatisfaction with this state of affairs on the return journey than at any other time. They set out excitedly with high ideals and return home exhausted and often dissatisfied. A *brancardier* described his experience in these words:

> After the pilgrimage you're tired, weary, jaded like I am now. You think: What is it all for? Was it worth it? I've got gout and swollen knees. After the pilgrimage you feel like a piece of wet rag. But you forget all your troubles and look forward to next year. It's like a child getting near Christmas or birthday, you can't wait to get back on that train again.

THE HANDICAPPED CHILDREN'S PILGRIMAGE TRUST (HCPT)

The HCPT pilgrimage is an example of a type of pilgrimage unique to Lourdes. Pilgrimages of this kind have three essential features. First, they are run by a full-time charitable organization which utilizes a high publicity profile amongst Catholics in the United Kingdom in order to raise funds. Second, they specialize in taking only one category of sick pilgrim to Lourdes, and the meaning of the term 'sick' is expanded to include the handicapped, retarded, mentally ill, those who suffer the disabilities of old age, and so on. Lastly, all those who are not sick pilgrims are helpers, so that the pilgrimage is structured around an intense involvement with disability for those able-bodied pilgrims who assist.

The HCPT makes an annual pilgrimage to Lourdes in the week after Easter. In 1985, when I travelled with them, over 4000 helpers, children, nurses, priests, and doctors travelled by air, rail, coach, and ferry to Lourdes. This immense number of pilgrims was divided into 'family-style' groups, each containing a nurse or doctor, a priest, and approximately equal numbers of helpers and children. The helpers pay their own fare and the children travel free. The helpers tend to be younger and are drawn more frequently from the middle classes compared with the pilgrims travelling with diocesan pilgrimages such as that from Liverpool.

I travelled with one of these small groups. The helpers in the group were from different parts of England and did not meet apart from this annual event. With one exception, the helpers were practising Catholics (one was a practising Anglican engaged to another helper). The two oldest members of the group were aged 30 and had been making the pilgrimage every year since joining as 16-year-old schoolboys. However, the children were unknown to the helpers before the actual journey. They met the group immediately before setting off for Lourdes; they waved goodbye to parents and friends and set off with a group of strangers. Parents are discouraged from accompanying the children. Most were non-Catholic. Their disabilities ranged from deafness to polio to spina bifida with complications; one boy was severely disabled by cerebral palsy.

By the time we had travelled from Westminster Cathedral to Dover, the immediate physical needs of the children had established the initial bonds between helpers and children which began to build up a cohesive group. The children were washed, fed and entertained by the helpers. Helpers did not relate to the children as parents, teachers, or authority figures, but rather made every effort to enable each child to express and fulfil their desires. The only things forbidden to them were those that were dangerous. The effect of this union of helper and handicapped child is all the more extreme when it is realized that much of the journey takes place in public. On board the ferry, the crew and passengers stared in amazement as literally hundreds of mentally and physically handicapped children, each with their own assistant, participated in wheelchair races in the corridors, explored the decks, the lifeboats, and the cafeteria, and waved, ate, cried, slept, and sang as the boat sailed to Calais. Some children had musical instruments, some toys, and most wore coloured hats which denoted their group but which also marked the scene as one of festivity and celebration.

The journey was thus marked not only by the presence of handicap *en masse* in a public place but also by its chaotic and carnival-like atmosphere (the word 'carnival' is particularly appropriate here, combining as it does the ideas of celebration and the breaking of taboo). On the journey, the coach, the motorway, the roadside café, the ferry, and the train station were all sites for a passing carnival of human disability. The hospitals, schools, institutions, all the hiding places of the deformed, retarded, and handicapped had been emptied out and their inhabitants swept triumphantly through places normally indifferent to their existence. It was as though a new order had been unleashed from the margins of society. In this way the pilgrimage to Lourdes was as much a journey into handicap and physical disability as it was a movement through time and space.

The two new helpers in this group had had almost no direct experience of handicapped people before the pilgrimage. Yet by the conclusion of the journey they had expanded their vocabulary of handicap and, through conversations with the regular helpers, had learnt the causes of cerebral palsy and could recognize the overt signs of spina bifida and hydrocephalus. They had become adept at performing certain nursing tasks indispensable for the care of the children, and had largely overcome any initial repugnance they might have felt for this unfamiliar and intimate involvement with the abnormal body.

This journey into handicap was continued and intensified at the shrine itself. The children stayed with the helpers in a hotel. Although the helpers insisted that 'the children are not sick – they're handicapped – so they don't stay in the hospital', they identified themselves as 'pilgrims who help the sick'. It was also said that the helpers were pilgrims but that they wanted the children to enjoy the journey as a holiday; the children, by implication, were not seen as pilgrims.

A description of some of the mundane details of daily life at the shrine will show something of the extent to which the involvement with physical handicap is central to this pilgrimage.

Each morning began with the helpers bathing and dressing the children and assisting them in their slow descent down to breakfast. Helpers had an average of about five hours sleep a night. Only one child could bathe and dress herself. The most severely handicapped girl would shriek and scream for no apparent reason and needed constant reassurance. No attempt was ever made to rush her. Helpers chose her clothes from the suitcase packed by her mother. They matched her shirts and trousers and sweaters and brushed and plaited her long hair. Then she was escorted slowly down to breakfast where another helper prepared special food for her and helped her eat it (sometimes the helpers had no time for their own breakfast). Another of the girls, badly deformed by spina bifida, was of normal intelligence and more sensitive than most teenagers about her appearance. She would lie on her side watchfully while a helper held up each of the garments in her suitcase for inspection; a long discussion would ensue about the relative suitability of the items for the day's activities.

One day, the group went for a picnic to the place where St Bernadette, the visionary of Lourdes, had worked briefly as a shepherdess. The site lies about 100 yards up a steep muddy path made slippery at that time by rain. All the food, cups, plates, knives, medicines, rugs, children, and wheelchairs had to be carried up this path. Helpers slipped and fell in the mud, wheelchairs became entangled in the exposed roots of trees, yet the delicate bodies of the children were handled with a fine degree of care, and frayed tempers were soothed almost instantly – one mistake could injure a child. The physical and mental strain was immense, but the helpers then had to spend the rest of the day preparing food, feeding the children, and entertaining them. The helpers were exhausted and elated at the end of the day, and sat drinking in a café after the children had gone to bed at 9 o'clock.

It is significant that, although cures at the shrine were mentioned occasionally by the regular helpers, it was only the new helpers who spoke unprompted of miracles in relation to the actual children on this pilgrimage. In each of these cases, it was with reference to the expectations of the children's parents. The more experienced helpers reassured them that miraculous cures were not expected by the parents, while the guidebook used by the group also made the point more than once that miracles were not a motivation for the pilgrimage. Helpers did believe in miracles, but they were spoken of historically or as having happened to other people. In other words, new helpers entered a structure where the expectation of miracles was suppressed.

This suppression was sustained during the pilgrimage in a number of ways. First, the absence of a kinship or prior personal tie between helper and child meant that the helper did not desire a cure for the child to the degree evidenced by the close relatives of other sick pilgrims whom I interviewed on other occasions. Second, the age of the children meant that their own desire to be relieved of their physical suffering was not as long-term and intense as that of an adult. Third, while the helpers understood a Lourdes miracle as a healing of sickness, they described the children as handicapped rather than as sick. Fourth, the pilgrimage itself was centred on the care of the suffering body: helpers spent far more time in this type of activity than they did participating in the rituals and activities of the shrine.

The pilgrimage thus had the effect of deflecting the desire for a miraculous cure from Our Lady of Lourdes and replacing this with an affirmation of the value of physical suffering. The children were encouraged to bear their suffering 'cheerfully', because it made them Christ-like. 'Real miracles' were said to consist of eliminating sin, and it was the expiatory role of physical suffering which was given the most explicit emphasis. When the children were taken into the baths, they were told that they were doing this because Our Lady requested it, and the cold, penitential nature of the experience was stressed; miracles, cures, and ameliorations were not mentioned.

Like the Liverpool pilgrims, the helpers were critical of themselves and the pilgrimage on the journey home. Some had had only two or three hours' sleep for the past few nights. The children, by contrast, were much more uninhibited than on the outward journey, and were in high spirits. When the parents met them at Westminster Cathedral, they noticed the change immediately. 'Stop dragging your feet!' said one mother to her child as they walked to the car. This child was noticeably less in command of her handicap than when she had set out. Perhaps the liberation of handicap had been too successful.

A COMMERCIALLY ORGANIZED PILGRIMAGE

This pilgrimage was a six-day journey by coach to Lourdes, Nevers, and the Rue du Bac in Paris. The London-based company which organized it advertised itself as 'a pilgrimage specialist'. A priest accompanied each of its pilgrimages, and a courier travelled with the group and took care of the daily arrangements. Most of the forty-six participants on this pilgrimage had first heard about the company through its advertisements in *The Universe*, a weekly Catholic newspaper; the priest was also recruited in this way. The average age of the group was about 48. They referred to themselves as pilgrims, and brought with them an impressive array of pious objects. Although there were many members of the group who sought a cure or amelioration for some physical ailment, this pilgrimage was not organized around the care of a group of sick or handicapped people, as were the two discussed above.

The party was composed of individuals or small groups of practising Catholics, together with one Pentecostalist. Lourdes was the most important of the shrines visited. Nevers was valued as the site of the incorrupt body of the visionary of Lourdes, while the Rue du Bac was known principally as the originating site of the popular devotion of the Miraculous Medal.

The primary identity of Lourdes for these pilgrims was constructed around miraculous healings and the presence of the sick. It was assumed that sick pilgrims would be present in great numbers and that they would be accorded especially privileged treatment by the healthy. In a pilgrimage such as this one, where no formal means of doing so existed, the treatment took the form of pilgrims performing small courtesies for the sick or disabled people whom they encountered at the shrine, and demonstrating a heightened degree of awareness of their presence and needs in conversation amongst themselves. In a confrontation with the courier over the poor quality of the hotel, one woman who had not been to Lourdes before made an impassioned speech before the assembled group, maintaining that pilgrims must protest to the company who had organized the pilgrimage because, 'We must make sure this never happens to sick people. We must make sure that invalids are never put into a hotel like this.'

Two men on the pilgrimage presented frequent problems for the group. One was an elderly man from London suffering from senility. He was travelling alone and often forgot which town or country he was in, what time to meet back at the coach, or where his hotel keys were. The other was an Irishman residing in Birmingham who was an alcoholic and drank from morning until bedtime. He also smoked a particularly potent variety of cigar. When dealing with the problems presented by these two, the other pilgrims expressed the idea that it was inappropriate to complain too much or even at all, since the men were 'sick' and because this was a pilgrimage to Lourdes. They would praise those who helped these people. The man seated next to the Irishman on the coach was frequently praised for his tolerance and forbearance.

The incorrupt body of St Bernadette at Nevers made an extraordinary impression on the pilgrims. They spoke as though they were in the presence of a Lourdes miracle. The body was never spoken of as 'it' but rather as the living saint herself: the physical perfection of the body was taken as evidence of a victory over death.

It was assumed that both the senile man and the alcoholic, together with the other pilgrims who were visibly unwell, were seeking a cure or amelioration from the pilgrimage. These assumptions were expressed quite unambiguously – for example, 'He's no doubt hoping for a cure'. A middle-aged woman from King's Cross, who described herself as ill, was always conspicuously close to any statue or object which the courier identified as being associated with miraculous cures. At St Pé, for instance, she ran her hands over various parts of the statue of Our Lady of St Pé and then touched the corresponding parts of her own body, as though she were attempting to 'put on' the perfect body of the statue.

It can be said, then, that although the sick were absent as a category organizing the group at the level of practice, they were nevertheless present for the group empirically as individuals and as a category at the level of consciousness. A woman said that she was not sick but she had come to pray for 'healing for all and especially for the sick'. She metaphoricized the concept of healing and thereby extended its range of meaning: all forms of imperfection were referred to in terms of the image of physical suffering.

THE PLACE OF THE SUFFERING BODY IN THE PILGRIMAGE CONTEXT

In the first two pilgrimages described, the presence of the sick pilgrims served to unite a group of near strangers into a single, concrete group. In both, this was achieved in a very literal way, through the construction of supernatural discourses around the meaning and value of the suffering body. By contrast, the pilgrimage without a concrete category of sick pilgrims lacked the unitary identity of the other two pilgrimages despite the strong desire of these pilgrims to make the journey a real pilgrimage and to participate as a group. Nevertheless, these pilgrims too recognized a sacred value in the suffering body encountered at the shrine. They went out of their way to make personal contact with sick pilgrims at the shrine, and their conversations revealed a concept of the sick pilgrim as being closer to the sacred and hence more valuable.

In each of the three pilgrimages, this notion of the proximity of the sick pilgrim to the sacred comprises two elements. On the one hand, the sick may be the object of a Lourdes miracle because such miracles are quintessentially miracles of physical healing. On the other hand, the sick are located within a discourse which sanctifies physical suffering (and through this, all suffering) by drawing upon the figure of Christ in the Passion and thereby redefining suffering as a form of sacrifice. These meanings of physical suffering were differently emphasized on each of the three pilgrimages. The Liverpool pilgrimage gave explicit recognition to each but the priests in their sermons and the lay helpers in their care of the sick more actively propagated the sacrificial meaning of physical suffering. The HCPT pilgrimage promoted the sacrificial meaning, even going so far as to deny in the guidebook the value of the miracle discourse altogether. The commercial pilgrimage recognized both discourses but the pilgrims and the courier expressed greater enthusiasm for the miracle discourse.

Interviews with sick pilgrims at Lourdes during the summer of 1984 revealed that 'healthy' pilgrims of all nationalities approach and treat them in a way analogous to the way saints are treated. The 'healthy' asked the sick to pray for them or for those close to them; the sick were given small gifts and pious objects, and were spontaneously stroked and caressed by strangers; they were requested to attend various rituals at the shrine in the company of 'healthy' pilgrims whom they had not met before; and they were massed together at the front of rituals and were generally accorded a favoured treatment in all areas of the town. The pilgrim at Lourdes who is identified as suffering physically is treated and often explicitly identified as being closer to the sacred than is the 'healthy' devotee. He or she is therefore approached as a mediator between this world and the next. In this sense, sick pilgrims can be said to perform the role of saints.

THE BODY IN CATHOLIC AND PROTESTANT DISCOURSES

So far, I have shown how physical suffering constructs the approach to the divine at Lourdes. I want to suggest by way of conclusion that this particular emphasis on the body is not exclusive to the Lourdes pilgrimage but is, rather, a unique characteristic of Catholicism. In order to present this case, I briefly consider certain teachings of the Catholic church centred on the body and compare these with certain practices in the Protestant tradition.

Today, the Catholic church still opposes most forms of 'modern artificialism' which assert the will of the individual over the reproductive function of the body.[4] The controversial papal encyclical *De Humanae Vitae* (1968), which reasserted the church's opposition to the use of contraception, noted the 'stupendous progress in the domination and rational organization of the forces of nature' which now enables men to exercise unprecedented control over their bodies and which raises the question of whether 'the transmission of life should be regulated by their intelligence and will rather than through the specific rhythms of their bodies' (Horgan 1972: 34). It goes on to approve only those methods of contraception understood to be based on the natural rhythms of the body. The justification for all this is that the fertility or the natural infertility of the human body reveals the will of God in the form of natural law. The reproductive cycles of the body are, in effect, God in nature.

For many Catholics today, especially the younger English Catholics amongst whom I worked, opposition to contraception is no longer an affirmation of created life but rather a subordination of the entire person to the reproductive function of the body. The reason why the church has adhered to this position in the face of strong opposition from within its own ranks can be inferred, I would hypothesize, from an examination of its teachings on other issues. These teachings manifest its staunch fidelity to forms of divine eminence attacked and discarded by the Protestants during the Reformation.

The Catholic church, for instance, teaches the Real Presence of Christ in the consecrated host: the communicant actually consumes the body and blood of Christ. Implicit here, and in the teachings on human sexuality and reproduction, are the ideas that the divine is embodied in, and that spiritual relationships are founded through, the human body. Human reproductive life reveals the divine. In this respect, human generation follows the pattern of the Incarnation, for both express a harmonious unity of divinity and flesh. The Catholic mass replicates this pattern again, on a higher plane: the host itself regenerates the communicant.

The Protestant churches do not teach the Real Presence. Their teachings on the body, however, reveal two extremes. On the one hand, there are those of modern Seventh Day Adventists, who enthusiastically embrace modern artificialism and run hospitals with advanced research facilities. On the other hand, there are groups such as the Christian Scientists, who refuse medical treatment altogether. What underlies the two positions is the devaluation of the body relative to the soul: if the body is devoid of divinity, it is a fitting subject for the improving efforts of the soul or it must submit absolutely to the divine. The Incarnation as image or process is absent in both the Protestant communion rite and in the teachings concerning the human body.

I wish to suggest, then, that there is an analogy between the teachings about the body of Christ in the communion rite and the teachings concerning the human body in its reproductive function. The Catholic church emphasizes, indeed insists, on the incarnate form of the spirit. The human body is *par excellence* the form of divinity in the world, a belief also evidenced in the veneration of saints' relics. However, it is the incarnate form in its unificatory power which is stressed in this analogy. The communicant consumes the body of Christ and is united with God; the church teaches that human reproductive capacity must be governed by divine rather than human authority, in order that kinship relations are simultaneously human and divine. It is the resulting human grouping in each case in which divinity is found. Protestant teachings, by contrast, emphasize the separation of body and soul and the superiority of the latter over the former.

Each of these varieties of Christianity also enjoins contrasting reproductive practices for its religious specialists. Within the Catholic tradition, priests and monks are celibate and celibacy is valued above the reproductive sexuality of the married laity. These categories are opposed as two orders of people, as sacred and profane, spiritual and bodily. The body/spirit dualism operates not only internally, as a recognized division within the person, but also externally, between defined social classes. In the Protestant tradition, however, where clergy are encouraged to marry and have children, the two classes of specialists and laity have been fused, and the vital principle is located within the person alone. In this sense, the Protestant tradition again denies that the body can be united with the spirit. The body is no longer sacred but, like nature itself, open to rational control.

NOTES

I am grateful to the Central Research Fund of the University of London and for the award of a University of London Postgraduate Studentship in order to finance the research upon which this chapter is, in part, based. I should also like to thank Dr Jonathan Parry, who supervised my doctoral thesis.

1 It is commonly assumed that pilgrimages, shrines, and apparitions are chiefly to be understood as the stuff of folk religion. Yet Kselman's work and my own on the history of Catholic pilgrimage to Lourdes suggest that the church has repeatedly used such phenomena to convert or to re-Catholicize populations. These histories show how the church at all levels has actively embraced and propagated devotions to shrines and apparitions. Further regional historical

studies of post-Reformation Europe are needed to tell us more about the relationship between the church and such devotions.

2 One of the pilgrims was miraculously cured on this first pilgrimage. His name was Jack Traynor and his story is the subject of a Catholic Truth Society booklet which is still sold throughout the United Kingdom. His cure has never been officially recognized by the church but most English Catholics refer to it as miraculous. Many Liverpool pilgrims on the pilgrimage described here had personally known Traynor. When I asked the priest, the spiritual director of this pilgrimage, why the diocese had made this an annual event, he told me the story of Jack Traynor and said, 'That clinched it for us really'.

3 I have elsewhere described this tension as one between miracle and sacrificial discourses (Dahlberg 1987).

4 I borrow this term from Dumont (1986). The title of the chapter is also taken from this same work. While I have reservations about the level at which the author conducts his analyses here, his particular understanding of the concept of holism has much to recommend it to those concerned with understanding the cultural construction of the body in the European context. His earlier work (Dumont 1980) contains an analysis of the problems a society espousing an egalitarian ideology encounters when it seeks to understand a society which values hierarchy. It is possible to see these same themes writ small in relation to the pilgrimages described in this chapter: many English Catholics have wondered if the sick pilgrims are empowered by their public and symbolic identity at Lourdes or if their individuality is crushed by taking on the desires of the collectivity. For another illuminating discussion of this same problem of the relationship between the part and the whole, but in quite another context, see Baumann (1987).

REFERENCES

Baumann, G. (1987) *National Integrity and Local Integration: The Miri of the Nuba Mountains*, Oxford: Clarendon Press.

Carlen, C. (ed.) (1981) *The Papal Encyclical*, vols. III and V, New York: McGrath Publishing Co.

Chaudefaud, M. (1981) *Lourdes: Un Pèlerinage, Une Ville*, Aix-en-Provence: Edisud.

Dahlberg, A. L. G. (1987) 'Transcendence of bodily suffering: an anthropological study of English Catholics at Lourdes', unpublished Ph.D. thesis, London School of Economics, University of London.

Dumont, L. (1980) *Homo Hierarchicus: The Caste System and its Implications*, trans. M. Sainsbury, L. Dumont and B. Gulati, Chicago: Chicago University Press.

———— (1986) *Essays on Individualism: Modern Ideology in Anthropological Perspective*, Chicago: Chicago University Press.

Horgan, J. (ed.) (1972) *Humanae Vitae and the Bishops*, Shannon: Irish University Press.

Kselman, T. A. (1978) 'Miracles and prophecies: popular religion and the church in nineteenth-century France', unpublished Ph.D. thesis, University of Michigan.

Rinschede, G. (1986) 'The pilgrimage town of Lourdes', *Journal of Cultural Geography* 7(1): 21-34.

Chapter two

Order and power at Lourdes
Lay helpers and the organization of a pilgrimage shrine

John Eade

INTRODUCTION

Lourdes, as one of the most famous shrines in Christendom, has stimulated a vast literature which has provided many insights into the religious life of the shrine and the activities of its pilgrims. There is one area, however, which has received scant attention: the role of the lay helpers (*brancardiers* and handmaids), who mediate between the higher echelons of the cult hierarchy and the pilgrims themselves. The prime aim of this chapter is to further our understanding of how the cult operates through the work of this crucial stratum of officials, and to demonstrate how, despite the tight control which the shrine exercises over its devotees, the structure of authority is such that there remains a certain flexibility in devotional beliefs and practices.

My interest in this topic stems from personal involvement as a *brancardier* during the last twenty years. On many occasions, I have been struck by an inherent contradiction within the role of lay helper. Although *brancardiers* and handmaids are required to help others, they also give commands to pilgrims, who are exhorted by their own pilgrimage leaders to obey. The ever-present tension between facilitating and denying the aspirations of others is sometimes expressed in brief, but emotionally charged, contests between lay helpers and pilgrims, as the latter challenge the practices and procedures established by the shrine organizers. Although the freedom of the pilgrims to express their individual wishes is considerably limited, many of them attempt to resist the power of the organizers in a variety of ways as they seek to impose their will over the proceedings.[1]

Although Lourdes may appear superficially to be a highly organized shrine, where helpers, 'ordinary' pilgrims, and religious and medical specialists collaborate smoothly within an integrated structure, the contests at the primary interface between pilgrims and lay helpers reveal a range of contradictions – between facilitating and denying, between power and resistance, and between collective order and freedom for individual expression. While the Turners cite Lourdes as an instance of communitas in Christian pilgrimage (Turner and Turner 1978: 230), the shrine actually demonstrates the co-existence of numerous oppositions. Indeed, as Sallnow notes in his approach to pilgrimage in a very different cultural context, 'the most helpful, pre-analytic image to hold in mind is of a tangle of contradictions, a cluster of coincident opposites' (1987: 9).

I will explore this contradictory character of Lourdes by concentrating on the activities of the male lay helpers (*brancardiers*) like myself. In this male-dominated shrine – where, ironically, two women (Our Lady, Christ's mother, and the visionary St Bernadette) are honoured,[2] the handmaids are primarily restricted in the public areas of the shrine to the female section of the baths. My admittedly male-oriented account will focus on the relationship between *brancardiers* and other pilgrims at two locales within the shrine precincts – the baths and the esplanade – where official practices and boundaries concerning the sacred are most prominently displayed and, at the same time, called into question.

THE ORGANIZATION OF THE SHRINE

The foundations of the shrine's organization were laid within twenty-six years of Bernadette Soubirous' apparitions at the grotto outside the old town. In 1866, eight years after the apparitions, the local bishop invited the Garaison Fathers, members of a revivalist missionary order established at a nearby Marian shrine, to lead the religious ceremonies in and around the grotto. In the same year the railway finally arrived at Lourdes, enabling pilgrimages to come from further afield than the immediate Bigorre area.

As the numbers of pilgrimages and day visitors increased, so the business of helping the sick and organizing the large crowds became more urgent. In 1881, a year after the first French National pilgrimage, an association of lay helpers was established, known as the Hospitality of Our Lady of Lourdes. The male founder members came from the higher echelons of French society – the first act of Hospitality charity was performed by Count Roussy de Sales – and the Order was modelled on a medieval foundation, the Knights Hospitallers of St John, which was originally established to care for the sick in Jerusalem (Cranston 1988: 66–8). As Lourdes developed into an international shrine, the Hospitality council, which provides its 'senior management', became less socially exclusive. Nevertheless, councillors from outside France are usually fluent in French, and the council presidents (all males) have been drawn from higher status French Catholic families.

The *brancardiers* and handmaids play the most visible and extensive role in organizing pilgrims, both at the shrine itself and at the major points of arrival and departure. As Dahlberg's account reveals, lay helpers also accompany the sick pilgrims on the organized pilgrimages, so that their influence extends far beyond the confines of the shrine itself. Their voluntary services include helping at the hospitals and hostels where sick pilgrims are accommodated, and at the station, airport, and major centres within the *domaine*.

The work of the Hospitallers from diverse nations is co-ordinated by a permanent bureau at Lourdes which directs their duties in and around the shrine and keeps in touch out of season with the numerous Hospitality branches throughout the world. These branches build on community ties and social clubs, which are particularly strong in urban working-class parishes. Lay helpers may also visit pilgrims whom they have met through their visits to Lourdes, especially the sick and handicapped. Contacts on a broader scale are also established through the annual meetings of the national Hospitality organizations, where senior Hospitallers discuss issues of mutual concern and information from the central bureau.

At Lourdes, some of the Hospitallers come under the direct control of the central bureau and are allocated jobs which complement the work of the lay helpers who accompany the sick pilgrims to and from the shrine. My own pilgrimage, for example, consists on average of forty to fifty helpers who work solely under the direction of the central bureau for a week. The group arrives during the last week of July, when many of the British pilgrimages are in Lourdes. The group does not include any sick pilgrims. Some of its members may not even travel with the main body of the pilgrimage, which usually flies out to Tarbes-Lourdes airport. The pilgrimage thus lacks both close contact with the sick, which is a feature of the Liverpool and HCPT pilgrimages described by Dahlberg, and the communal ties which link helpers in some pilgrimages between visits to the shrine.

Members of the pilgrimage are directed by the central bureau to various duties, primarily at the station, the baths, the grotto, and the esplanade. The period of service is called a *stage*, and *stagiaires* are distinguished from their colleagues on the organized diocesan pilgrimages, for example, by the different coloured lines on the braces (*bretelles*) which Hospitallers are required to wear while on duty. Service under the central bureau is generally accorded higher status among Hospitallers, and those who wish to become senior helpers within the diocesan pilgrimages frequently perform *stages* before the arrival of their own group.

The division of labour between the two types of *brancardier* is not rigid, however, since both can help anywhere when not required for some specific duty. Yet the Hospitallers who travel to and from Lourdes on the Liverpool or HCPT pilgrimages are clearly in far more intimate contact with 'ordinary' pilgrims than are the *stagiaires*. Their pilgrimage experience is usually more intense and they are less influenced by the attitudes and procedures of senior Hospitallers within the central bureau.

The leaders of the central Hospitality have emphasized from the beginning the importance of discipline combined with charity and piety. Many of the Hospitality's critics have argued that Hospitallers have become obsessed with discipline and with the maintenance of a complex hierarchy of military-style levels of command. To become a full member of the Hospitality, for example, volunteers have to perform a number of *stages* which are recorded by the central bureau. *Stagiaires* are then welcomed into the Hospitality at a special mass, where they are awarded bronze medals signifying their appointment as auxiliary members (*auxiliaires*). After completion of several more *stages*, the *auxiliaires* are awarded a silver medal at the 'Medal Mass' and become full members of the Hospitality (*titulaires*).

Hospitality members thus constitute an officer cadre which is used to co-ordinate and direct the work of the trainee volunteers. Some are responsible for certain areas, such as outside the baths or the grotto. Comradeship among the Hospitallers is encouraged through the meals which are provided at the Abri St Michel, the Hospitality hostel within the *domaine*. Members of the council sit at the top table during these meals and usually move on to an adjoining office to discuss orders for the following day.

The military discipline is supposed to go hand in hand with religious discipline. While on duty, *stagiaires* are formally required to pray when free to do so. They have to set an example to others, and their actual handling of those whom the Hospitality describes as 'the sick' must demonstrate their commitment to charity, the third principle espoused by the organization. Given such high ideals, the frequent indiscretions by individual *brancardiers* and handmaids provide further ammunition for the critics of the Hospitality system.

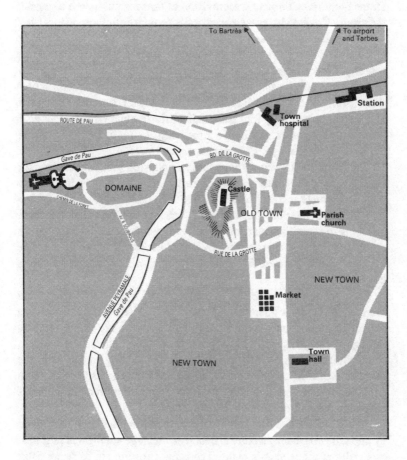

Figure 2.1 Map of Lourdes: the domaine and the town

THE BATHS AND THE PROCESS OF HEALING

The spring which Bernadette Soubirous uncovered during one of her visions quickly became associated with miraculous cures. Bernadette took very little interest in stories about these cures, but her apparitions have nevertheless long been used to establish a link between the spring and healing.

The commercial exploitation of the spring was pre-empted by the shrine authorities through the provision of taps for public use alongside the grotto. Covered baths were eventually provided for those who wished to wash in the spring water. These buildings sheltered pilgrims from the elements and also guaranteed them a degree of privacy and decency. More recently, a much larger structure has been erected to the south of the grotto. Most bathers now have to pass the grotto first, and frequently stop to pray there before the altar and statue of Our Lady of Lourdes. However, although approximately four and a half million people visit Lourdes each year,[3] only a small proportion visit the baths. In 1980, 399,547 pilgrims did so, and of these about 70 per cent were female.

The baths are housed within a long, single-storey building facing the Gave river and the meadow (see Figure 1.1). The building is divided into male and female sections, and in each section three doors admit pilgrims into the bath interior. Outside, long benches are provided for those queueing to enter. Sick pilgrims usually wait outside the first door and are accorded priority so that they can be bathed as quickly as possible. Inside the men's baths there are five cubicles for adult males and one for young boys.

Each section of the baths is cordoned off by metal barriers, and *brancardiers* mount guard at the gates which lead directly to the area outside the doors. Only certain categories of pilgrim are allowed to pass through these gates: the sick, priests, nuns, Hospitallers, and children under adult supervision. All other bathers are expected to queue, using the benches provided. A *brancardier* is stationed outside each of the bath doors so that he can regulate the flow of pilgrims into the cubicles following orders from those in charge inside.

A highly stratified division of labour, therefore, has been developed by the staff at the baths in order to deal with the large numbers of pilgrims, especially at the women's baths. The task of sorting out different categories of pilgrim is undertaken at the gates of each section, and during busy periods the *brancardiers* work under considerable pressure. This is most intense outside the gate to the women's section when the queue has been closed well before the end of the two-hour session. The decision to stop the queue is officially explained in terms of the need to release the helpers for rest and lunch after the morning session and to make room for the Blessed Sacrament procession, which follows the afternoon's bathings.

Disappointed pilgrims denied access to the baths often vent their anger on the *brancardiers*. Some might not be able to return, especially those who are visiting the shrine for a short time. To them, the *brancardiers* appear to be officious, power-crazy, and hard-hearted, and they sometimes accuse the *brancardiers* of a lack of Christian charity – a wounding accusation given the Hospitality's formal commitment to charity and piety as well as to discipline. Some resourceful pilgrims use the hierarchical structures to their own advantage by appealing, if they belong to organized pilgrimages, to their own priests and lay officials for help. In such instances, decisions may be referred to the senior *brancardiers* and, ultimately, to the head of the section inside the baths.

All these various activities and pressures make for a lively atmosphere. Amid the busy comings and goings during a hectic session, the staff attempt to establish a modicum of prayerful calm. The waiting pilgrims are exhorted to join in the recitation of the rosary, for example, through a powerful public address system which is clearly audible within the baths. The language used for the prayers usually depends upon which organized pilgrimage has brought its sick pilgrims to be bathed. During each session several languages can be employed as different groups arrive and depart.

The formal ritual at the baths constitutes an attempt by the officials to ensure collective worship among people who come from diverse social and linguistic backgrounds. Their efforts meet with only partial success, however, and there is frequently an animated buzz as pilgrims await their turn to enter the baths. While everyone is encouraged to join in the prayers and hymns, those who do not speak the language engage in their own prayers or talk among themselves about issues which may frequently have little to do either with bathing or with the pilgrimage.

When pilgrims do discuss bathing, they often express concern about what is going to happen to them. Where does one go once inside? What clothes does one remove? How does one get dry? How cold is the water? Will people speak my language? How long will it all take? Answers to these questions can be sought from other pilgrims in the queue or from *brancardiers* who are working outside the baths. This undertow of conversation is overlaid by the public prayers, and on busy days there may be repeated calls for silence if the conversation is deemed too loud by the officials.

The apprehensions of the waiting pilgrims provide some indication of their vulnerability. Queueing in all sorts of weather and with all kinds of people adds to the tensions of a situation where pilgrims are particularly sensitive to the actions of others, especially the lay helpers. Many pilgrims do not appreciate the *brancardiers*' overriding concern for order and regulation. Sometimes a carnival atmosphere develops as pilgrims sing, pray, and chat with their companions in order to defuse the tensions they are experiencing.

Outright conflict between *brancardiers* and pilgrims usually erupts over demarcations concerning space and time, and between the sacred and the secular. Closing the session early frequently causes considerable frustration, as already mentioned. Anger can also be triggered by the rules concerning who can gain direct access to the area outside the baths. A child accompanied by an adult, for example, can be allowed through the gate leading straight on to the favoured area. Other companions might want to accompany the child but are frequently told to join the long queue.

The rules therefore encourage various forms of subterfuge, such as the presentation of official-looking documents purporting to give access to the area. *Brancardiers* are told to accept only those who bring a 'sick card' (*carte de malade*), but unless *brancardiers* and pilgrims speak the same language the decision to reject other cards and documents might appear unreasonable to the frustrated pilgrims.

Brancardiers themselves are sometimes irked by the complicated rules for differentiating between those who may enter by the front gate and those who may not. However, only a limited number of pilgrims can be admitted to the area outside the baths because of the way the space is arranged. Most of the area is kept clear for the reception of sick pilgrims, and there are only a few benches available for queueing bathers. If the gate-keepers allowed too many exceptions to the rules of entry, the area would become overcrowded and reprimands might be delivered to the senior Hospitaller in charge.

The many rules devised by the Hospitality concerning the organization of space outside the baths are related to regulations in operation throughout the *domaine*. One of the most annoying regulations for visitors concerns dress. The shrine staff employ Guardians, police look-alikes posted at key locations to ensure propriety and security. Scantily dressed pilgrims on hot summer days may be reproved by these Guardians, and similar disapproval may be expressed by *brancardiers* at the baths. An extensive etiquette concerning respectful behaviour is implemented in the sacred space of the *domaine*, and particular care is taken to preserve the dignity of places imbued with especial sacredness such as the baths and their environs.

Many pilgrims, however, do not share the officials' definitions of respectful behaviour, and considerable tension can be generated when *brancardiers* insist on their understandings of propriety. For pilgrims, the sacredness of place does not have to be sustained by so many rules and boundaries: they desire to be in immediate contact with it and become frustrated by procedures and barriers which keep all but a select few at a distance.

Despite the impressive organization established at the baths, the process of waiting one's turn must be understood in terms of diverse practices which are not neatly integrated into a uniform structure. Pilgrims pursue their own strategies, occasionally in defiance of those set up by the *brancardiers* and priests. Although leaders of organized pilgrimages may encourage their colleagues to observe official regulations at all times, pilgrims often refuse to obey Hospitallers who frustrate their plans. Pilgrims are not docile bodies subject to the control of others: they can and do resist the power of the organizers – within limits – in order to attain their own objectives.

INSIDE THE MEN'S BATHS

On the basis of my experience of working inside the male section of the baths, I shall describe the variety of practices involved in the bathing and the strategies pursued by the pilgrims. Again, a high degree of co-ordination is achieved, but both *brancardiers* and pilgrims are able to follow their own procedures to a certain extent. Indeed, on occasions, pilgrims enjoy a considerable amount of freedom to shape the bathing process according to their own individual wishes.

Once inside, the pilgrims sit on low benches along a corridor running along the whole length of the bath. The baths themselves are contained within cubicles which are shielded from the corridor by blue and white curtains. Each cubicle is divided into a front section, where pilgrims undress down to their underclothes and hang their clothes on hooks or place them on the chairs provided, and a rear section containing the bath, which is entered down some steps with enough space on either side for *brancardiers* to help the bather.

Each bath is attended by six to eight *brancardiers*. Two help the pilgrim undress and keep the flow of bathers running smoothly. Two more take up positions on either side of the steps leading to the bath. The bather goes to one of these *brancardiers* who takes him behind a curtain so that he can remove his underpants and have a cold, damp towel placed around his midriff. Each pilgrim is then taken to the top of the bath, where he can pray. He is then led down the steps into the water and up to the end of the bath by two other helpers, who hold him on either side and take him backwards into the water. The assistants then help the pilgrim to his feet, inviting him to kiss a small statue of Our Lady and to say a brief concluding prayer. The bather walks back upstairs and returns to the cubicle where he has left his clothes. The pilgrims are reminded by the organizers of their pilgrimages, and also by the *brancardiers*, that they should get dressed without drying themselves. Once dressed, they are guided out of the cubicles by the helpers.

This description is obviously schematic, since practice in each cubicle varies according to the changing personnel and the different rules established by the various senior *brancardiers* responsible for the bath section during the season. Moreover, pilgrims often insist on doing things their own way, and considerable flexibility is required of *brancardiers* if they are to accommodate the needs of particular bathers. Helpers have to be mindful of the dangers of a routinized efficiency where bathers are processed as quickly as possible, especially during busy periods. Indeed, reforms introduced during the last ten years reflect official concern at the way in which efficiency can stifle freedom of expression. There has been an increasing sensitivity to the vulnerability of the pilgrims and a recognition of the rawness of what amounts to a severe physical ordeal for many people. *Brancardiers* are now encouraged to give pilgrims more time for reflection, and procedures have been introduced which call for more communication between bathers and helpers.

A decade ago, for example, the standard practice was for the bather to walk straight down the steps and up to the end of the bath, where he would be required to kneel down in the water and recite from a large card a lengthy series of prayers, both in Latin and in his own tongue. He was then immersed so that his whole body, including his head, was briefly under water. After immersion, bathers were frequently invited to drink the water, and a small cup was provided for this purpose.

Current procedures represent a substantial modification of these practices. Rather than repeat a strict formula of prayer in the water, the pilgrim is first invited to reflect upon the sacrament of baptism before going down into the bath. Waiting pilgrims are similarly exhorted during the broadcast prayers to recall their own baptisms. Moreover, inside each cubicle are signs reminding bathers of the way in which baptism incorporates them into a church of fellow believers.

After pondering the significance of baptism, the bather is usually invited to pray for his own intentions. When he is taken to the end of the bath he is asked whether he wants to be completely immersed or to have his head left above the water. *Brancardiers* will also leave pilgrims to bathe themselves if they so wish, but remain in attendance in case they are needed. No reference is made to drinking the water, but the pilgrim is still invited to kiss the statue of the Virgin after immersion.

These changes reflect the movement from miracle to sacrificial discourse, described by Dahlberg. The new procedures depend far more upon communication between the bather and the two assistants who receive him at the top of the bath steps. During late July, for example, the *brancardiers* are predominantly from France, Britain, and Italy, but the baths can expect to receive people not just from these countries but also from Belgium, the Netherlands, Spain, West Germany, Luxemburg, Malta, and Poland. The helpers must first establish the national identity of the bather, and then negotiate some medium of communication. If no linguistic commonality can be found, sign language is used or prayers are said by the helpers in their own language in the hope that the pilgrim will follow suit. Any attempt to convey the importance of baptism in such circumstances is useless, and the bather will probably be led down to the end of the bath after an appropriate period of silent reflection. Since the bather will have watched others going through the process while waiting his turn, immersion can usually be assisted by the use of sign language or gentle physical guidance.

Bathers, however, can insist on their own forms of devotion, and *brancardiers* are encouraged to be alert to pilgrims' wishes. Consequently, some bathers may follow some of the old practices, such as walking down to the end of the bath, kneeling in the water to say their prayers, and drinking the water. They may ask to be immersed several times, or demand that they be allowed to immerse themselves. Some pilgrims bring special objects to be bathed with them, especially rosaries. Some decide that the experience is all too much, and refuse to go down to the baths at all.

Other bathers, however, appear to be stunned by the whole process of bathing and welcome being speedily processed through the routine. It is often an empty formality to ask a bather to reflect meaningfully upon his baptism when he is suffering from a cold, has a damp towel around his waist, and is about to plunge into bitterly cold water. As helpers are able to bathe at the end of the session, I have frequently experienced the way in which the mind can go blank on such occasions and can appreciate the desire of pilgrims to be taken through the whole operation as quickly as possible.

The ability of bathers to mould procedures according to their individual wishes is most evident in the case of sick pilgrims. Many instruct the helpers about the manner in which they wish to be undressed and bathed. When they enter the bath they can be helped down the steps by the two helpers or taken into the water by four *brancardiers* on a stretcher or in a harness. Some bathers or their companions insist that immersion would be too much for them, and in such cases some form of sponging takes place at the top of the steps. The formula of prayers is also frequently dictated by the pilgrim's wishes, with most of the *brancardiers* in the cubicle joining in. Sick pilgrims who are so incapacitated that they cannot indicate what they want are treated with particular care. With such people, if they are not accompanied by their own helpers, bathing procedures are largely determined by visual clues concerning their wishes.

The ability of sick pilgrims to mould operations in accordance with their desires thus stems directly from their physical state. The baths are especially associated with the healing of the sick, and great care is exercised by the helpers in handling their bodies. *Brancardiers* are eager to ease the strain of undressing and bathing in the bitingly cold water, and are well aware of the danger of slipping on the marble and stone surfaces of the cubicles. In some cases, immersion is clearly a major achievement for the pilgrim, and the whole cubicle shares in the palpable sense of victory enjoyed by the bather.

The relief at having survived what is a considerable physical ordeal is also shared by other pilgrims who are not 'sick' in the official parlance. While the sick are treated like celebrities, the recent emphasis on the symbolism of baptism also draws attention to their fraternal equality with other pilgrims. The association of the baths with miraculous healing is now minimized, and the immersion of bodies is officially understood in terms of the purging of sins, membership of the church, the sacrificial offering of Christ's body, and his resurrection from the dead.

Nevertheless, as their prayers reveal, both 'sick' and 'healthy' pilgrims visit the baths in the hope of relief from personal troubles. Some sick pilgrims movingly beg to be cured during the bathing, and their helpers join in their prayers for the alleviation of their illnesses. Bathing the sick is a profound experience for *brancardiers*, and the atmosphere in the cubicles can become extremely intense. The official interpretation of bathing, then, is paralleled by the popular belief that a person might well be cured through immersion.

The organizers' attempts to create an atmosphere of tranquil prayer-fulness and reflection in the baths are invariably compromised. Frequently, there is much humour and teasing. Helpers will jolly sick pilgrims along, while sick pilgrims, in return, will joke about their infirmities. The problems of wet socks, shoes which will not fit on again, or the weight of an infirm person can all be the subjects of light-hearted exchanges. The fear of the cold water and the shock of entering it are also prime topics for amused reaction and discussion. *Brancardiers* will join in the fun in order to relieve the tension, especially during a hard, busy session. When a cubicle is not occupied, *brancardiers* are frequently tempted to joke amongst themselves about the national differences between them, their social backgrounds, their experience of Lourdes, and so on.

In sum, therefore, the baths involve a variety of practices which are not neatly co-ordinated through standardized official procedures. Indeed, the organizers encourage a flexibility and variety which was far less evident a decade ago. Given the diversity of languages and nationalities, the baths operate with remarkable efficiency. Yet the official emphasis on calm reflection and quiet is impossible to achieve entirely, given the large number of activities and instructions to which both bathers and *brancardiers* have to submit. There are many moments of good humour and fun in which even senior *brancardiers* may join, temporarily casting aside the mantle of serious-minded authority.

The men's and women's baths are subject to somewhat different pressures, however. Female bathers outnumber males by approximately two to one; consequently the queues for the women's baths are more strictly regimented, while the atmosphere inside is apparently more 'serious'. In the men's baths a more leisurely pace is feasible, and towards the end of a session some cubicles might receive very few pilgrims, permitting the *brancardiers* to take baths themselves and still cope with any late arrivals.

A further significant shift in bathing procedures over the last ten years or so has been a de-emphasis on the two female saints associated with miraculous healing at the shrine – the Virgin, invoked through the recitation of the 'Hail Mary' before descending to the bath and through the kissing of her statue after immersion, and St Bernadette herself. The current stress on the sacrament of baptism directs attention away from miraculous cures and towards the institutional authority of the church and the redemptive sacrifice of Christ. The shift from miracle to sacrificial discourse implies a shift from a focus on the female, virginal, and maternal elements symbolized by the two female saints and towards a preoccupation with the Son of God and with the male, fatherly qualities of the hierarchical institution of the church.

RELIGION, MAGIC, AND OFFICIAL INTERPRETATIONS OF BATHING

Shrine officials have always been careful to draw a sharp distinction between religion and magic at Lourdes, especially in the context of the baths. An authoritative French guide-book, for example, explains the symbolic importance of the baths with reference to the sacraments of reconciliation (through confession) and the eucharist:

> This water is not magical: it is drinkable, chemically pure, similar to other springs at Lourdes, lacking in therapeutic or radioactive qualities. It sometimes heals but its role is primarily to remind us that we should turn also to Him who is the source of eternal life.
>
> (Billet and Lafourcade 1981: 170, my translation)

Indeed, according to this guide, there are two healing springs at Lourdes – the one uncovered by Bernadette and the church's spring which 'consists of the sacraments of Reconciliation, the new Baptism, and the Eucharist, the food of eternal life' (ibid).

In another official guide, drinking the water in the baths is dismissed in the following terms: 'It is good mountain water, pure and drinkable. In the baths it is polluted by the sick who pass through it, but the Virgin never said that one should drink that water' (Alaux, Joulia and Billet 1977: 20).

At the same time, it is obvious that individual bathers, whether 'healthy' or 'sick', come to the baths in the hope that the actual experience of immersion in the waters will effect some transformation in their fortunes or the fortunes of those close to them. Bathing takes on an instrumental rather than a purely symbolic quality. Careful attention is paid to material objects, such as the water itself and the statue of the Virgin. Indeed, the personalities intimately associated with the baths, Christ's mother and the young peasant visionary, provide a more tangible and expressive focus for the bathers' reflection than do the more abstract concepts of sacramental graces proposed by the shrine's official interpreters.

The authorities have been ever-vigilant to stamp out any ideas concerning the magical properties of the water. For example, in the last few years, during late July, the French lay deacon who serves as the head of the men's section of the Hospitallers has brought the *brancardiers* together for a short ceremony in the central bath. Readings are taken from the gospels to reinforce the official view of the baths and their significance. On one occasion, a young *brancardier* scooped some water out of the bath in his cupped hands so that colleagues could dip their fingers in the water and bless themselves. He was stopped in his tracks by the head of the section, who claimed he was treating the water in a superstitious fashion. The water, he said, simply issued from a local spring and was not to be handled with any special care.

Current interpretations, then, consider the more spectacular aspects of Lourdes ceremonial to be less important than their spiritual value. According to Billet and Lafourcade, one of the contemporary features of Lourdes is the 'great desire for interiority' or inward reflection. The celebrations are now conducted in a new style – 'direct, concrete, immediately intelligible, without pomposity or pathos' (1981: 2). This more humane approach has undoubtedly influenced the Hospitality, leading to less formality and greater fraternity towards pilgrims and other Hospitallers.

Official understandings of the 'sick' have also changed. They are now seen far more as ordinary members of the church, united in their common sinfulness, their baptism, and their need for sacramental grace. As cures are played down, their endurance of suffering is emphasized and their significance as representatives of collective caring is underlined: 'Their presence at Lourdes is not a spectacle offered for piety or even for sympathy. Pilgrims like others, they want to be treated like others' (ibid: 166). This interpretation clearly ignores, however, the multitude of ways in which the sick *are* marked out as a spectacle, and the relatively small number of pilgrims who actually serve them.

The changes in practices in the baths, and the ideological representations set out by Billet and Lafourcade, constitute attempts to shift popular understandings away from the miraculous to the sacramental. 'Superstitious' beliefs and behaviours are to be eliminated from the sacred area of the baths, and official commentators and senior *brancardiers* should seek to enforce a rigid distinction between 'religion' and 'magic'. Yet inside the baths themselves, pilgrims and *brancardiers* do not necessarily recognize this distinction in quite the same way. A uniformity of meaning and practice across the different levels of the Hospitality organization is impossible to achieve. What actually emerges is a continually shifting mix between the older, popular beliefs and behaviours and the newer, official ones, between what is now classed as 'superstition' and what the authorities deem to be religion proper.

SELF-CRITICISM WITHIN THE HOSPITALITY

A persistent theme in the official reinterpretation of Lourdes is the emphasis on fraternal solidarity between all those involved at the shrine. Representations of this fraternal sentiment have built upon earlier images of the ideal Hospitaller. Hospitallers traditionally received a small handbook which explained their duties. Cranston notes that the handbook warned the new member to:

> be ready to bear cold and heat, sun and rain, hunger and thirst, and long waits. He must not exceed a walking pace when in charge of invalid chairs. He must not smoke when in charge of sick persons. He must know how to carry the sick so that they suffer the least possible jolting.
>
> (Cranston 1956, revised 1988: 67)

Last but most important: '*He must pray without ceasing*' (ibid).

Hospitallers are well aware that the reality is often quite different. Pilgrims frequently find them overbearing and megalomaniac, while Hospitallers are not afraid to voice their dissatisfaction with their own colleagues. The younger volunteers, in particular, resent the military aspects of the Hospitality and its hierarchical organization.

Sometimes, such dissatisfaction is voiced publicly. The Secretariat of the Hospitality of Our Lady of Lourdes in England, Scotland and Wales, for example, included in its 1987 newsletter a swingeing attack on Hospitaller behaviour. The author spoke of declining standards in the organization and expressed his sorrow at:

> the lack of sensitivity among my fellow *brancardiers*, the lack of courtesy, the lack of good manners, the lack of brotherhood, a degree of selfishness, not understanding, or even trying to understand, the international aspects of the Hospitalité and the services they perform. Only self-interest! For example, 'My pilgrimage', 'My *stage*', 'My group'.

The author explained the insensitivity of his colleagues generally in terms of both self-interest and also the sectoral fragmentation of particular groups at the shrine. He then proceeded to describe the attitudes of *brancardiers* which caused most offence:

> Grumpy, theatrical, egotistical, self-important *brancardiers* who man-handle pilgrims into position, *brancardiers* who snap their fingers for attention or to show direction. *Brancardiers* who lack the time and the courtesy, simple seconds to answer a request politely, and if not

knowing the answer at least trying to solve it. *Brancardiers* who lack patience and understanding of people of other nationalities....

These failings were related to the speed with which the helpers sought to fulfil their obligations:

> *Brancardiers* at various places and duties, who seem to be working on a bonus system, where speed is of the essence and humanity is non-existent, but it only takes a few more seconds!

This trenchant critique highlights some of the problems which have already become evident in the discussion of bathing. The individual needs of pilgrims are frequently ignored by the organization, which tries to maintain a military-style discipline where everyone is involved in the giving and receiving of orders. Although impressive numbers of pilgrims can be processed at a centre such as the baths, there is a cost: the *brancardiers'* concern for a speedy and efficient service can encourage them to ignore the particular interests of individual pilgrims.

The author of the critique also highlights the differing interests among *brancardiers* and the autonomy of levels within the hierarchy. The vision of international communitas at a fraternal, Christian shrine inspires many pilgrims both inside and outside the Hospitality organization, but, at the same time, pilgrims are vividly aware of their national and linguistic heritages and differences. The countervailing forces of nationalism and internationalism deeply influence Hospitality procedures and practices, making for an uncomfortable tension on many occasions. Even where groups of workers are drawn from the same country, other alliances and differences come into play, especially those based on social class. These particularistic ties co-exist with the impressive shows of international solidarity which are such a feature of the shrine. Such particularism leads to fragmentation and to a diversity of practice which the central Hospitality both implicitly encourages and discourages, through its recognition of national solidarities on the one hand, and its call for sisterly and brotherly co-operation on the other.

A continual interplay of opposing forces, therefore, is a major feature of the Lourdes pilgrimage. The shrine and its lay helpers are involved in a permanent tension between universalism and particularism, hierarchy and equality, uniformity and fragmentation, discipline and freedom of expression. The consequences of this tension for relations between Hospitallers and pilgrims are vividly displayed in the *brancardier's* criticisms quoted above, which are undoubtedly shared by a number of his colleagues. More consideration by the *brancardiers* themselves is proffered as the solution. Critics of the Hospitality organization, however, fail to appreciate that tensions and conflicts are inherent at a shrine where opposing forces are continually being acted out, either in dramatic public rituals or in more private devotional procedures such as those at the baths.

One major problem which the critique fails to mention is the inequality between males and females at the shrine. Lourdes celebrates the devotional experiences of a young peasant girl and the intercessionary role of the Virgin Mary, and 68 per cent of its pilgrims are female. Female helpers, however, come into their own only in the women's section of the baths, and in the hospital. Their representatives on the Hospitality council are heavily outnumbered by the male *brancardiers*, and the ritual celebrations at the shrine are orchestrated by the religious hierarchy – which is exclusively male – and senior *brancardiers*. Admittedly, social boundaries between male and female Hospitallers are now beginning to weaken as the council starts to 'move with the times'. Female helpers are now allowed to join their male colleagues and eat together in the Hospitality dining room in the Abri St Michel, for example. Yet such changes have not been accompanied by any increased power-sharing, nor by the provision of a wider range of jobs for female helpers outside the baths.

The tensions which are evident at the shrine are, of course, shaped by forces within the wider society. The cult dramatically represents these forces in its rituals, which express the influence of national, linguistic, class, and gender differences. We have already seen these forces at work in the context of the baths. An even more vivid manifestation is provided by one of the most important celebrations at the shrine – the procession of the Blessed Sacrament from the grotto to the esplanade, which takes place every afternoon after the baths have closed.

THE ESPLANADE AND THE PROCESSION OF THE BLESSED SACRAMENT

The esplanade is a large, open area to the east of the grotto. It faces the cliff out of which the grotto was carved, and also the two churches which have been built beside and on the cliff itself, the two basilicas of the Rosary and the Immaculate Conception. Imposing staircases lead from the esplanade up to the church and crypt of the Immaculate Conception, providing fine views of the *domaine* and of the town beyond.

The esplanade was laid out early in the shrine's career in order to cater for the large demonstrations of faith and healing, particularly those during the French National pilgrimage. Organized pilgrim groups can hold their own ritual celebrations at the chapel of St Bernadette, in the south-west corner of the esplanade, while larger ceremonies can be conducted on the platform which overlooks the esplanade, in front of the Rosary basilica. It is against this platform that most organized pilgrimages have their group photographs taken before leaving the shrine.

To the east of the esplanade, a wide avenue sweeps up to St Michael's Gate, punctuated only by the statue of the Crowned Virgin, which roughly marks the boundary of the esplanade, and the Crucifixion statue near the gate itself. On either side of this avenue are major institutions and religious centres – the Acceuil Notre Dame hospital, the Medical Bureau, the Pius X underground basilica, the St Joseph chapel where the Hospitality's 'Medal Mass' takes place, and the Hospitality hostel, Abri St Michel.

The esplanade and the avenue are used to most dramatic effect during the Blessed Sacrament and torchlight processions. Those wishing to participate in the former assemble at the grotto and walk westwards towards St Michael's Gate, before turning back towards the esplanade along the other side of the avenue. On arriving at the esplanade, pilgrims move to various parts of the arena, leaving space for sick pilgrims who are waiting in rows on either side. Responsibility for placing people within the esplanade is assumed by a senior *brancardier* together with other Hospitallers on duty there.

The climax of the ceremony is the arrival of the Host carried in a monstrance by one of the senior visiting clergy. The Host is taken slowly along the lines of wheelchairs and stretchers. The clergy then proceed up to the platform in front of the Rosary basilica, where the entire congregation is blessed with the Host. When the Host has been taken into the Rosary chapel the participants disperse, with long lines of wheelchairs and stretchers moving off to the various hospitals – the Acceuil Notre Dame and the Acceuil St Bernadette in the *domaine* and Our Lady of Seven Sorrows in the town.

The procession graphically represents the unity of the church and the diverse elements which that unity is supposed to incorporate. Each individual pilgrimage is heralded by its flags and banners proclaiming the national origins of the various dioceses and parishes which constitute the party. A few groups, however, display the particular institutional or medical character of their sick pilgrims, such as that of the Handicapped Children's Pilgrimage Trust described by Dahlberg and the special French pilgrimage in early July which caters for those crippled by polio.

The flags and banners are paraded down the middle of the esplanade, which is left clear during the course of the procession, and up the stairs to either side of the Rosary basilica. They are followed by the emblems of the various international Catholic lay solidarities, such as the Legion of Mary. Behind the Host and the clergy in their solemn procession around the esplanade come the visiting doctors from the various organized pilgrimages – visible demonstration of the élite status accorded to the medical profession by the cult and of their deep involvement in its operation.

Recent changes in the Blessed Sacrament procession reveal a degree of relaxation in the maintenance of rigid boundaries both between *brancardiers* and pilgrims, and between 'sick' and 'healthy' participants. The esplanade is now treated less like a parade ground to be kept clear of all but a select few. Organized pilgrimages are encouraged to take their sick pilgrims on the procession, so that the arrival of the various groups at the esplanade becomes less of a patronizing visitation by the able-bodied of the serried ranks of invalids, as it tended to be in the past. In addition, the use of vernacular languages has encouraged greater participation in the hymns and prayers by diverse national groups, although the Latin chant, *Tantum Ergo*, is still used for the final act of devotion before the Host is returned to the basilica.

The public celebration of unity, however, co-exists with the inevitable conflicts and tensions between Hospitallers and pilgrims. While more participants are now allowed access to the 'front stage' of the esplanade, *brancardiers* are still required to keep the crowds behind the lines of sick pilgrims on either side of the arena, and tension can easily be sparked off as the ceremony reaches its climax.

The *brancardiers*, who are allocated to permanent duty at the esplanade during their *stages*, are responsible for clearing the area for the procession and supervising the placement of the sick in lines for the blessing. When the invalids arrive, there is hectic activity as they are moved into position. Helpers and healthy pilgrims alike are required to keep clear of the area assigned for the sick, and *brancardiers* experience considerable difficulty in keeping the various categories of participant apart during busy periods. Pilgrims might not appreciate the necessity for staying clear of certain areas, particularly when there is little space for standing or sitting. In the summer heat, seating in shaded areas is highly prized and pilgrims sometimes refuse to abandon 'occupied territory'. Once again, *brancardiers* are seen to be heartless, officious guards who push people about with no regard for individual needs.

During the Blessed Sacrament procession, therefore, space becomes highly contested, as Hospitallers and pilgrims jockey for position. Since the *brancardiers* are heavily outnumbered, they rely on persuasion and their official status to defend the space which has been marked out by their senior officials. As the ceremony approaches its climax, the boundary between sick and healthy pilgrims becomes ever more difficult to maintain, as the faithful press forward to catch sight of the Host and of the clergy following the priest conferring the blessing. Such moments of intense religious fervour dramatically illustrate the uneasy co-existence of communitas and status, of solidarity and self-interest, which is so characteristic of the cult as a whole.

Although official accounts of the shrine do lay stress on the occurrence of cures during the Blessed Sacrament procession, the healing is expressed in terms of the sacrificial rather than of the miracle discourse. The low-key approach discourages the kind of dramatic displays common during late nineteenth- and early twentieth-century pilgrimages to Lourdes. Marnham, drawing on Emile Zola's account, highlights the role of the clergy during one such pilgrimage in commanding the sick to overcome their ailments through faith:

> The supreme moment of this confidence trick, in the most positive sense of that phrase, occurred in 1897, which was a papal jubilee year. When the French National had completed the Blessed Sacrament a papal benediction was bestowed on all present. One thousand priests chanted the *Confiteor*, then the leader of the pilgrimage, an Assumptionist, turned on the sick and *ordered* them to believe, to prove their faith and to stand up and walk. Amid a terrible silence, first one and then another did this, until 'forty-one poor wretches' had left their crutches and stretchers in triumph and rejoined the healthy race. The enthusiasm of the crowd on that occasion became a danger in itself.
>
> (Marnham 1982: 124)

This description is supported by Benson's account of the ceremony in 1908, the year of the shrine's fiftieth anniversary:

> I saw a sudden swirl in the crowd of heads beneath the church steps, and then a great shaking ran through the crowd; but there for a few instants it boiled like a pot. A sudden cry had broken out, and it ran through the whole space ... hands clapped, voices shouted: '*Un miracle! Un miracle!*'... And then again the finger of God flashed down, and again, and again; and each time a sick and broken body sprang

from its bed of pain and stood upright; and the crowd smiled and roared and sobbed.

(ibid: 125)

These accounts bear little relation to the scenes I have witnessed over the last twenty years. If sick pilgrims do hope for a miraculous cure, they are certainly not encouraged by the clergy to 'stand up and walk'. The crowds surrounding them are controlled by the Hospitallers, and they are enjoined to participate in the hymns and prayers in a reflective manner. Although official discourse makes mention of 'the sick', the emphasis is on the commonality of all believers: all pilgrims are exhorted to reflect on their need for sacramental grace, absolution from their sins, and conversion to the life of a pure believer.

When a cure does appear to have taken place, the *brancardiers* are under instructions to whisk the person away to the Medical Bureau. Marnham describes the case of a young French pilgrim, René Scher, who in 1966 regained his sight during the procession. As he grew aware of the multitude around him:

he became frightened and told the man next to him that he could see and that he was afraid. Immediately the man took his cue and, displaying the instinctive joyous reaction of the devout pilgrim, began to shout, '*Il peut voir!*' 'He can see!' The *brancardiers*, following their usual instructions in such cases, then hurried the boy away from the gathering towards the offices of the Medical Bureau, where the gates were locked against the crowds.

(ibid: 126)

Rather than encourage the kind of crowd hysteria described by Zola and Benson, *brancardiers* are now used to quash any such stirrings and to control the reactions and emotions of the pilgrims. Any spectacular event has to be treated with great caution, and the person concerned has to be quickly extracted from the throng for the cautious and lengthy medical examination devised by the Bureau. Through these means, the shrine's officials seek to rebut the widespread scepticism which now surrounds allegedly miraculous cures, both inside and outside the church.

Despite the changes in official attitudes towards miraculous cures from the beginning of the century to the present day, sick pilgrims are still subject to tight physical control by the shrine organizers. They might not be summoned from their stretchers and wheelchairs, but they are lined up along the esplanade and taken along the processional route in carefully demarcated sections by their helpers. Nevertheless, it is they who are in closest proximity to the Host during the blessing, and it is they who still have the capacity to disrupt the smooth order of the proceedings with an allegedly miraculous cure – an event all the more significant now, perhaps, for the rarity of its occurrence.

The power of the sick, both during the procession and in the baths, as mentioned earlier, resides in their physical state, in the visible sign of their ill-health and suffering. Dahlberg has likened their role during the pilgrimage to that of saints, in that they are believed to enjoy a privileged access to the sacred. Yet their status in this respect is ambivalent and compromised, perhaps more so today than in the past. They are publicly shown to be special, yet the rituals also lay stress on their common humanity as well as their equality with other members of the church. The blessing of the sick encourages the hope that someone might be cured, but care is also taken to remind people that suffering must be patiently endured and that no release should be expected from either physical or mental illness. The individual aspirations of sick pilgrims are acknowledged, but they are at the same time incorporated within the collective prayer and worship of all participants.

The occasional eruption of the transcendent through the healing of a particular pilgrim challenges this official stress on universalism and commonality among pilgrims, both sick and healthy. It is as though the thin crust of discipline and order is torn asunder by the volcanic explosion of the supernatural forces which the clergy have themselves invoked. On such occasions, the other principal actors in the drama, the *brancardiers* and the crowd, occupy contrasting positions. The *brancardiers* are employed by the officials to restore order by removing the individual who has disrupted the smooth flow of events and immediately delivering the person for investigation by medical experts. Many people in the crowd, however, do not wish to take such a detached view; instead they react with enthusiasm and intense curiosity, since the event appears to validate both the prayers they have been uttering during the procession and the widespread belief in shrine-induced miracles.

CONCLUSION

The organization of lay helpers at Lourdes is clearly a powerful instrument in the hands of the shrine organizers for maintaining what they define as order and orthodoxy in such public arenas as the esplanade and the baths. While the shrine provides a ritual space where the diverse meanings and practices of the various pilgrims might be expressed and manifested, its highly organized structure imposes severe limits upon such diversity. The helpers are required to implement official discourse and practices, to encourage 'correct' behaviour at all times, and to impose strict boundaries around sacred space and time. Lourdes, in fact, provides a striking illustration of the manner in which religious enthusiasm can be at once stimulated, channelled, controlled, and curtailed by an internally differentiated and hierarchical cult officialdom.

The power of the helpers to direct pilgrims into certain areas and procedures encounters resistance from certain pilgrims at least. Boundaries which *brancardiers* seek to maintain around sacred space become the sites of conflict as pilgrims attempt to shift, break down, or circumvent official limits and routines. These contests are most evident in such public zones as the esplanade and the area outside the baths. Inside the men's baths, by contrast, there is more opportunity for pilgrims to express their individual wishes and to pursue their own strategies.

Yet the power of pilgrims to resist the authority of lay helpers and other shrine organizers must not be over-emphasized. Even inside the men's baths, where flexibility and sensitivity to pilgrims' needs are most evident, the pilgrims' abilities to shape bathing procedures to their own designs have depended largely upon changes initiated by Hospitallers themselves. Helpers are prepared to criticize the insensitivity and officiousness of their colleagues, but changes in official practice have emanated from the higher echelons of the Hospitality and not, it seems, in direct response to criticism from the lower ranks, or from local confrontations between junior Hospitallers and pilgrims.

The Hospitality itself is not a neat, integrated, hierarchical structure which dominates the pilgrims absolutely. Each level of the organization enjoys a certain autonomy, and junior members do not necessarily agree with their senior colleagues. Indeed, the differences in interpretation of rules and procedures provide room within which pilgrims can manoeuvre. This diversity of meaning and practice is apparent, for example, in the differing significances attached to the miraculous. The official movement away from miracle to sacrificial discourse has yet to impress those *brancardiers* and pilgrims who actively entertain the possibility of miraculous cures. The rigid distinction which senior officials make between 'religion' and 'magic' is also ignored by many helpers and pilgrims.

Gaps in communication between helpers and pilgrims also limit the neat integration of official practices. Such gaps can help pilgrims to mould bathing procedures according to their own wishes, but they can also lead to friction between Hospitallers and pilgrims outside the baths and during the Blessed Sacrament procession, as *brancardiers* strive to prevent people from crossing official boundaries.

What we see at Lourdes, then, is the dynamic interplay between structure and the communitas upon which Turner placed so much emphasis. Indeed, the presence of other contrasting elements – power and resistance, collective discipline and freedom of expression, hierarchy and equality, sacred and secular – offers further illustration of the 'cluster of coincident opposites' which Sallnow noted in his study of pilgrimage in the high Andes of Peru.

This oppositional interplay, however, takes place within an overall context of inequality. The balance between structure and communitas is heavily weighted towards structure. Although pilgrims can resist the power of Hospitallers, their victories are few and most do not even consider challenging official rules. The very fact that my account of order and power at Lourdes is based largely on my experience as a *brancardier* points to another aspect of institutionalized inequality – the dominant position held by male helpers within the Hospitality and the confinement of female workers to relatively secluded locales within the shrine.

What I have considered here is the way in which a particular kind of order is maintained by male helpers through the exercise of their power, a power which is contested by pilgrims to a limited extent and which is constrained by a lack of integration between institutional levels, by breaks in communication between staff and devotees, by different preferred devotional practices, and by inconsistent modes of interpretation. The dominance of *brancardiers* is thus by no means absolute and uncontestable, since diverse meanings and practices manage to co-exist even at this, perhaps the most highly organized of Catholic pilgrimage shrines. Nevertheless, the degree to which visitors can express and realize their desires at Lourdes is tightly constrained by the boundaries around space, time, and the sacred which the *brancardiers* are obliged to preserve.

NOTES

1 Although I note with interest Foucault's discussion of power, resistance, and knowledge (Foucault 1977, 1979; Gordon 1980), I do not attempt a Foucauldian analysis here. I do not, for example, adopt his 'non-possessive' approach towards power. Moreover, the practices and discourses concerning the body which I examine here cannot be simply incorporated within the disciplinary technologies explored by Foucault.

2 The association between male domination within the Roman Catholic church and official discourses concerning Our Lady has been examined by Warner (1976).
3 The Bilan Touristique give a figure of 4,608,000 for 1987.

REFERENCES

Alaux, J., Joulia, P. P., and Billet, J. M. (1977) *Lourdes*, Turin: Editions du Cerf.

Bilan Touristique (1988) '*Lourdes 88 Retrotel*', *Bilan Touristique de la Saison 1987*, Lourdes: Mairie de Lourdes.

Billet, B. and Lafourcade, P. (1981) *Lourdes Pèlerinage*, Paris: de Brouwer.

Cranston, R. (1988) *The Miracle of Lourdes*, New York: Image Books.

Dahlberg, A. (1987) 'Transcendence of bodily suffering: an anthropological study of English Catholics at Lourdes', unpublished Ph.D. thesis, London School of Economics, University of London.

Foucault, M. (1977) *Discipline and Punish: The Birth of the Prison*, London: Penguin.

_____ (1979) *The History of Sexuality, Volume 1: An Introduction*, London: Penguin.

Gordon, C. (ed.) (1980) *Power/Knowledge: Selected Interviews and Other Writings 1972–1977 by Michel Foucault*, Brighton: Harvester Press.

Marnham, P. (1982) *Lourdes: A Modern Pilgrimage*, New York: Image Books.

Sallnow, M. J. (1987) *Pilgrims of the Andes: Regional Cults in Cusco*, Washington, DC: Smithsonian Institution Press.

Turner, V. W. and Turner, E. (1978) *Image and Pilgrimage in Christian Culture: Anthropological Perspectives*, Oxford: Basil Blackwell.

Warner, M. (1976) *Alone of All Her Sex: The Myth and Cult of the Virgin Mary*, London: Weidenfeld and Nicolson.

Chapter three

San Giovanni Rotondo and the shrine of Padre Pio

Christopher McKevitt

INTRODUCTION

Students of pilgrimage have generally, and logically, focused on pilgrims. They have sought to understand the motivations and experiences of those who make a journey to a place believed to be important in the quest for salvation. Of less interest has been the place itself to which the pilgrims travel, even where that place exists as a community independent of its sacred status. The literature, then, is largely silent on those who live in the vicinity of places considered sacred.[1]

It is my aim in this chapter to present a wide-angle lens view of a community which now derives its economic livelihood and much of its self-identity from a pilgrimage movement which has been based there for approximately sixty years, although the town itself traces its origins to prehistoric times. The town is called San Giovanni Rotondo, and is famous in Italy and throughout the Catholic world for the shrine of Padre Pio da Pietrelcina.[2] I intend to consider San Giovanni Rotondo as a pilgrimage centre not so much from the point of view of the pilgrims but mainly from that of the residents of the town itself.[3] These I divide into two categories. First, there are the Sangiovannesi, the people whose town owes much of its present character to a 'saint' they recognize as their own.[4] Second, there are the resident devotees, those outsiders (*forestieri*) who have come to live in the town because of their devotion to Padre Pio.[5]

This particular focus of my research owes something to a remark made to me a few days after my arrival in San Giovanni Rotondo, by one of the Capuchin priests who run the shrine. My aims were initially not precisely formulated and I explained to the priest that I had not yet decided whether pilgrims or the townspeople were to be the subjects of my research. The priest replied that I ought to decide quickly, since neither group had anything at all to do with the other.

In fact, before undertaking fieldwork, I had assumed that the local people would show indifference towards the saint and his shrine. Yet this priest's insistence that in San Giovanni Rotondo there were, in effect, two distinct communities, independent of each other, was not the whole story. It soon became apparent that such a notion, articulated by many people I met in the course of my research, was only partially correct. The problem I wanted to address was this: what is it that makes San Giovanni Rotondo sacred, for whom does this quality obtain, and how is it maintained?

ABOUT PILGRIMAGE

The concept of the sacred is central to the literature on pilgrimage. It is axiomatic that a pilgrimage is a journey to a sacred place which lies beyond the mundane realm of the pilgrim's daily experience. Students of pilgrimage have variously considered this sacred place to be the cosmic centre (Eliade 1959), the world behind this world (Christian 1972), or 'a sacred periphery which suddenly, transiently, becomes central for the individual, an *axis mundi* of his faith' (Turner and Turner 1978: 34). As well as being a literal journey, pilgrimage is a journey of the religious imagination. Here I assume, with the Turners, that pilgrimage can be thought of as 'exteriorized mysticism', the private, mystical journey made public, a journey of the spirit which is physically enacted. Although Victor Turner's model of pilgrimage has been justly criticized by many, including Morinis (1984) and Sallnow (1987), this concept of exteriorized mysticism is, I suggest, still useful; in fact, Morinis' own comment that pilgrimage can be 'an allegory of the journey of the soul to God' (1984: 297) is not too dissimilar.

The idea of pilgrimage as exteriorized mysticism alerts us to a major difference between the two categories of people I have defined. Mysticism is essentially a private, asocial activity, in that the mystic is one who endeavours to forsake the world. But there is always a tension inherent in the mystical endeavour. Invariably, the mystic is drawn into the very social relations which he wishes to eschew by those who see him as a useful conduit to supernatural power. Yet that quality also sets the mystic apart from ordinary men and women. Those who are not set apart, but seem to be imitating the mystic in some way, are problematic. Exteriorized mysticism in the form of pilgrimage, therefore, cannot be readily comprehended by those not undertaking the journey. As I show later, this problematic, boundary-crossing feature of mysticism is one which is all too evident in San Giovanni Rotondo.

The sacred is not a given or something fixed, but must be constantly created and recreated. A conscious effort is required on the part of the pilgrim to use the appropriate symbols, myths, and rituals in order to vivify the experience of pilgrimage and to make real the sacredness of the place. Given the necessity of the journey and the concomitant altered frame of mind, it might seem justifiable to assume that, without these, the sacred does not exist. It is this problem which I endeavour to address through the ethnography of San Giovanni Rotondo. I also suggest that, despite the usefulness of the Turnerian paradigm in some respects, attending more to the pilgrimage centre itself points to its limitations as a comprehensive model of the phenomenon.

Before examining the competing notions held about Padre Pio and his shrine, I present some background information on the town and its saint.

PADRE PIO: A BIOGRAPHICAL SKETCH

The figure of Pio remains a fascinating one, even if by now the intensively productive hagiographic industry complicates the task of anyone wishing to learn the 'true' story of this holy man. The compiling of one, generally agreed version is a process which is still under way. For my purpose here, though, the essential details are these.

Padre Pio was born Francesco Forgione in 1887 in Pietrelcina, a small agricultural community in the province of Benevento, southern Italy. He was from a devout peasant family, poor but not destitute. Pio's father twice emigrated for limited periods to work in South America and the U.S.A. By all accounts, the young Francesco was a pious child. His mystic experiences are said to have begun at an early age: he often saw the Madonna, and was also the victim of diabolic attack. At the age of 16, he entered the Capuchin order and was given the name Pio. At that time the most rigorous branch of the Franciscan family, the Capuchin order was noted for its austerity, its adherence to the rule of poverty, and the fact that the friars were all bearded as a sign of their ascetic lifestyle.[6]

The discipline and rigour of the Capuchin novitiate suited Pio, and he was soon recognized as a spiritually gifted person. His health, however, was poor, and his studies were often interrupted by periods of illness, although no satisfactory diagnosis could ever be made. Throughout his studies, it was feared that he would die prematurely before being ordained. A dispensation was granted (since according to canon law he was some months too young for ordination) and he was made a priest in 1910. At first, Pio continued to live with his family, where he had been sent to recuperate or die. The order then reclaimed him and he lived for brief spells in different friaries of the province. It was during this period that he began the spiritual direction of certain pious women known to his superiors. In 1916 he was sent for a time to the friary of Santa Maria delle Grazie in San Giovanni Rotondo. Here, in the cool air of the mountains and away from the malarial plain, his health seemed to improve a little.

PIO IN SAN GIOVANNI ROTONDO

The friary was then situated outside the village, and was reached only by a rough, 2-kilometre mule-track ascending the hill.[7] It had been founded in the sixteenth century but was by this time 'a place of desolation', having fallen into a state of disrepair following the changing fortunes of religious orders in the wake of the unification of Italy. It seems that contact between the friars and the Sangiovannesi was not intimate and was probably restricted to certain feast days associated with the miraculous image of Madonna della Grazie venerated in the friary church. There were only two or three other professed friars living there at the time. Pio wrote to his superiors:

> People rarely come to the church and deep silence surrounds me, all I hear from time to time is the sound of the little bell round the neck of some sheep which the shepherds take to graze on the mountain that rises behind the convent.
>
> (Alessandro da Ripabottoni 1983: 71)

After a few months away, Pio returned to the friary and was to remain there until his death.

San Giovanni Rotondo lies at 600 metres above sea level on the Gargano, the mountainous region known as the spur on the boot of Italy (see Figure 3.1). Throughout its long history it has always been, like so many other villages and towns of the area, a poor and isolated place.[8] When Pio first went to live there it was a community of about 11,000 *montanari* (mountain dwellers), who mostly made their living as shepherds, day labourers, or artisans. The poverty of the place is always stressed in the devotional literature, and is often accorded scriptural significance. Nevertheless, the impoverished conditions were real enough according to my informants and other evidence.

Once established, Pio undertook the spiritual direction of several local women and soon became known in the village as a holy friar. On 20 September 1918, he was praying before the crucifix in the friary church after mass when he had a vision. He described the experience at length in a letter to his spiritual director. There appeared before him, he wrote, 'a mysterious person' whose 'hands and feet and side were dripping blood.... The vision disappeared and I became aware that my hands, feet and side were dripping blood' (Pio da Pietrelcina 1980: 1217–18).

News of the stigmatization of Pio quickly became known in San Giovanni Rotondo, passed on initially, it seems, through the women to whom he acted as spiritual director. By the following spring, people of nearby towns in the region and from further afield had begun travelling to San Giovanni Rotondo to ask the holy friar for a 'grace' – a cure or some other favour. The Italian press began to carry reports of the 'stigmatized friar of the Gargano'.[9] The church authorities began to take a reluctant interest in this unknown Capuchin in the remote south of the country, and this interest was to continue and at times intensify to a serious degree throughout Pio's life.

CHARITABLE WORKS

Pio considered himself as one called to exercise a divine mission to save souls. He saw himself as suffering everything which Christ suffered during the crucifixion, and these physical sufferings, along with his mysterious illnesses, were, he believed, essential to this mission of co-redemption. Yet he also expressed concern for the material well-being of others, in particular that of the people of San Giovanni Rotondo. Following a period of civil unrest, which led to fatal clashes between socialists and fascists, Pio's advice was sought by local politicians. He encouraged reconciliation and lent his support to a programme of reforms which included the construction of roads, the improvement of hygienic facilities, and, importantly, the establishment of a small municipal hospital. Previously, the nearest hospital was some 40 kilometres away in the provincial capital of Foggia, and poor roads made the journey a difficult one. In this work of charity, Pio was assisted by certain lay collaborators, mostly members of the local Congregazione di Carità.

This first initiative failed for reasons which remain unclear, and the hospital was closed within a couple of years. Pio, however, was nurturing a more grandiose project. This was to be the Casa Sollievo della Sofferenza, the Home for the Relief of Suffering, a 500-bed hospital built with money donated to the stigmatized priest. The hospital was built, not in the village, but on a site near the friary, open land donated to Padre Pio by a local devotee. It was to be a place where doctors cured the body but where

Figure 3.1 Map of Italy, showing San Giovanni Rotondo

the spiritual welfare of the patient was also to be dealt with. Fund-raising involved many influential devotees of Pio, mainly non-Sangiovannesi, men and women with contacts in the outside world.[10]

The Casa Sollievo was officially opened in 1956 and was hailed as a remarkable achievement. Not only had sufficient money been raised, but the huge building had actually been constructed in this remote, inaccessible village. Employment had been provided for local people, for as much as possible had been constructed on the site. Plans were immediately announced for expansion, and Pio expressed the hope that San Giovanni Rotondo would become a *città ospedaliera*, a hospital city, where Christian doctors would engage in advanced medical research.

Other projects designed to improve life in the village were also begun by or with the blessing of Pio, including nursery schools, schools for the handicapped, and labour co-operatives. At every opportunity, it is reported, Pio urged visiting politicians to 'do something for these poor people'.

THE CULTING OF PIO

Meanwhile, the unofficial cult of Pio had been developing; indeed, it was the widespread devotion to him that had made his charitable ventures successful. The press, both Catholic and secular, frequently carried reports about him. Many of those who visited the holy man were local peasants, but there were also outsiders, foreigners, professional people, clergy, and members of the church hierarchy. Since the town is on an ancient pilgrimage route to the shrine of St Michael in Monte Sant'Angelo, pilgrims to the archangel's shrine would also visit Padre Pio *en route*.

The development of the cult, with all its vicissitudes and fierce controversies, is too complex to describe in detail here.[11] In summary, the church was characteristically wary of the personal following which the stigmatized priest attracted. Indeed, the hierarchy went further than the non-committal assessment customarily accorded to apparitions or other phenomena which stimulate popular movements. In an attempt to dampen popular enthusiam – described as 'fanaticism' – it was officially declared as early as 1923 that the phenomena attributed to Pio could not be regarded as having any supernatural origin (Pagnossin 1978: 176).

Pio seemed to become a focal point for the implicit and explicit criticism of local clergy, and the authorities were fearful of the power which the Capuchin might command. Twice Pio was effectively censured, and the faithful were expressly discouraged from making pilgrimages to San Giovanni Rotondo. Clergy in other parts of Italy were not only concerned about reports of fanatical behaviour and the extent to which Pio or his fellow Capuchin friars might be encouraging this personal cult, but they also resented the fact that funds were flowing out of their own dioceses into an unknown backwater in the deep south of the country.

At times, fierce battles seemed to flare up between the 'friends' and the 'enemies' of Pio, as the polemical writers label the two sides. More often than not, the enemies were those priests (including fellow Capuchins) and members of the hierarchy who seemed not to believe in the miracles attributed to Pio, who doubted his personal sanctity, and who disapproved of the vast following he had attracted. Yet by the time his death was approaching, the Capuchins in San Giovanni Rotondo had had a large new church built, with a place marked out in the crypt for the tomb of their special confrère.

In much of the literature, Pio emerges as a silent and suffering figure, one who submitted meekly to the will of his superiors even when they appeared to have misunderstood him. However, exactly what role he played in the rise of the popular movement is unclear; this, indeed, is one of the questions which the historical commission in the cause of his beatification has been charged to investigate.

'SAN GIOVANNI SI É FATT NA BELLA CITTADINA' – 'SAN GIOVANNI HAS BECOME A NICE LITTLE TOWN'

San Giovanni Rotondo has doubled in size and expanded far beyond the nucleus of picturesque houses which constitutes its 'historic centre'. Pio is usually credited with making the town what it is today. As one informant remarked, he achieved what no politician, local or national, had ever been able to do for the place. The two industries centred around him – the hospital and the pilgrimage – are largely responsible for the town's present wealth. Through these, jobs were created and services provided which otherwise might not have been available. As a result, there has been less emigration from San Giovanni Rotondo than from other towns in the region. Today, the town even boasts 'English-style' pubs and discotheques.

Padre Pio has not only put the town on the map; he forms the basis of the local economy. Sangiovannesi informants often used to tell me that if I wanted to imagine what their town would have been like today without Padre Pio, I had only to visit some of the other towns in the Gargano hinterland. It is true that many of these places do not have the outward appearance of prosperity that San Giovanni Rotondo has: one is more likely to see livestock being herded through the main street rather than hoteliers at the wheels of their four-wheel drive vehicles. The people of the neighbouring town of San Marco in Lamis are said to be particularly envious of San Giovanni Rotondo's good fortune: I once heard a young man from there describe Pio as 'manna from heaven' for the Sangiovannesi.

The mule track which once separated the village of San Giovanni

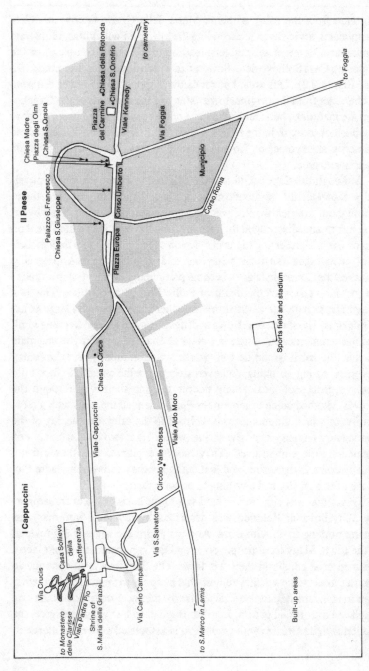

Figure 3.2 Map of San Giovanni Rotondo

Rotondo from the friary of Santa Maria delle Grazie is now the Viale Cappuccini, a wide avenue ascending the hill, lined with villas, shops, and a number of large modern hotels, leading to the shrine complex and the imposing Casa Sollievo della Sofferenza which dominates the entire town (see Figure 3.2). This area, known as the Cappuccini, is rather different in character from the original town. Many of the residents of the Cappuccini are *forestieri*, outsiders, who have come to work in the hospital, or to establish or to work in the hotels. Other *forestieri* and non-Italians came primarily as devotees of Pio and decided to stay. These also live in the Cappuccini area.

Although the Cappuccini and the original town are no longer physically separate, the residents make a clear distinction between them. Throughout my fieldwork, I was constantly surprised when Sangiovannesi informants dissociated themselves from the activities which went on 'up on the hill', referring to the promotion of the cult of Pio which in their eyes encouraged fanatical behaviour and aggrandized and materially enriched the Capuchin friars. I became particularly aware of such attitudes on the anniversary of the death of Padre Pio, 23 September. This is a solemn feast in the life of the shrine, and there is an especially large influx of pilgrims. The shrine overflows with devotees and visitors keeping vigil, and the ceremonies culminate in a mass at 2 a.m. Many of my young male friends told me it would be well worth a visit in order to see the 'crazy devotees' eating, drinking, and even sleeping in the church. In fact, I did observe groups of local young people making their way through the crowds who had come to remember Pio. I attended the vigil with a local family, of which the mother was devoted to the saint. On the day of the anniversary I again visited the shrine, where I met two local women who seemed a little embarrassed. They hastily explained that they did not usually come to the shrine, and that, although they believed in Padre Pio, 'none of this' really had anything to do with them.

This denial was puzzling. What I saw as the basis of life in contemporary San Giovanni Rotondo was described by my local informants as having nothing to do with them. And yet Padre Pio is generally revered in the town. Many local people do attend the vigil ceremonies or place a red memorial candle in their windows. The Sangiovannesi continue to regard Pio as their own: they remark that he spoke to them in dialect rather than in standard Italian. He is also clearly the local patron saint, having displaced the official patron, John the Baptist, and, to a lesser degree, the Madonna della Grazie (with whom Pio is associated). 'In every house in

San Giovanni Rotondo', I was told, 'you'll see an image of Padre Pio.' Most shops, bars, and public buildings also display an image of the saint. Nevertheless, the Sangiovannesi consciously attempt to distance themselves from the official cult and pilgrimage. These activities take place in the Cappuccini area. Townspeople remark that pilgrims 'never' come down into the town, although they must drive through it to reach the shrine.[12] They also claim that the friars know nothing of their affairs. The town and the Cappuccini are, it seems, two different worlds.

In order to understand this separation, no longer geographical but none the less strictly maintained at an ideal level, it is important to distinguish between Pio and the cult of Pio. While the saint himself is honoured by the Sangiovannesi, his legacy is more problematic. I turn now to an examination of this legacy, which I divide into two interrelated spheres: the material and the spiritual.

THE MATERIAL LEGACY

The attitude of the Sangiovannesi has to be explained with reference to the position of the material legacy in the local political economy. I sometimes heard the phrase, *'Qui i frati commandano'*, 'Here the friars are in charge' – a recognition of the fact that the local economy is based on the industries of the hospital and the pilgrimage. The Capuchins do not literally control the town; rather, they stand metonymically for all the successful claimants to Pio's legacy. The friars do, however, control the shrine. They possess the body of Pio, buried in the crypt of the new church of Santa Maria della Grazie. They also possess most of the relics of Pio, and preserve his cell as it apparently was on the day of his death. They promote devotion to Pio through an intensive production of literature encouraging pilgrimage to his shrine and belief in his intercessionary powers. They have prepared and presented the request for the beatification and canonization of their confrère. The work of friars posted to the shrine is solely to promote the message of Pio, and it is their monopoly of this enterprise which governs the perception of them by the townspeople.

The material legacy of Pio comprises two principal components: the pilgrimage industry and the hospital. In the eyes of the Sangiovannesi, the material benefits of both have eluded the townspeople themselves. The pilgrimage industry has successfully promoted San Giovanni Rotondo as a tourist town, necessitating the construction of hotels and other amenities for visitors. But the local people say that outsiders have monopolized this industry, claiming that, along with the flood of devotees, canny businessmen from elsewhere were attracted to the town in search of a guaranteed profit on their ventures.

The other component of Pio's material legacy, the Casa Sollievo della Sofferenza, forms part of the charitable foundation Opera Padre Pio, which was originally run by Pio himself with the assistance of a group of lay devotees. The question of ownership was always a thorny one. The Casa Sollievo was established as a charitable institution for the poor, but state bureaucracies require the nomination of an owner of land, buildings, and funds. Pio was dispensed from his religious vow of poverty so that he could manage the hospital. But to whom, in fact, did the hospital belong? To Pio, to 'the poor' of San Giovanni Rotondo, to the Capuchin order of which Pio was a member, or to the Roman Catholic church to whose hierarchy Pio was ultimately answerable? The issue became more urgent as Pio grew older and the future of the institution in the absence of its founder had to be considered. There was, on the one hand, the sociological problem of the transmission of charisma, and, on the other, the practical one of nominating worthy and reliable heirs. A political struggle unfolded, as various interested parties sought to realize their claims.

The possession wrangles which ensued towards the end of Pio's life and which continued after his death are too complex to deal with here. Suffice it to say that the Casa Sollievo is now owned and run by the Vatican, under the direction of a Vatican prelate. Although it remains a private concern, it is fully integrated into the national health system and has the status of regional general hospital. Development is ongoing: the hospital now has 1000 beds and employs 1700 people, of whom 300 are doctors working in twenty-two departments.[13]

In effect, as many Sangiovannesi told me, the Casa Sollievo is foreign territory within the Italian state. The same could be said of any number of church foundations in Italy, but here the technical foreign status of the institution has special significance. The townspeople claim that Pio built the hospital out of concern for their plight. Yet the Vatican – 'like the sea which always takes but gives back nothing' – derives great wealth from their hospital. The institution dominates the town both physically and economically, but its affairs are secret to ordinary folk in the town. Some individuals, however, do benefit from their private connections with the friars and with the hospital administration. For example, I was told that, whenever the hospital requires more land for expansion, it negotiates secretly with certain local politicians, and tracts of mountainside are exchanged for promises of jobs and other favours.

Whether or not these claims are correct, they nevertheless underline the notion that control of both the cult of Pio and of his charitable legacy has passed out of the hands of the Sangiovannesi. They express the feeling of having been alienated from the gift of Pio. No one denies that the town has derived enormous benefits, but it is said that the cult has brought disadvantages as well. Religious cranks are all too evident amongst the visitors. Development has been too rapid, with insufficient attention paid to environmental effects. And the gift has been appropriated by those who came with a pretended devotion but whose real motive was pecuniary profit. There is, indeed, an underlying notion of Pio's gift as a 'limited good', weakened and dissipated among an excessive number of claimants – some of them none too worthy of the benefits.[14]

THE SPIRITUAL LEGACY

The townspeople's sense of alienation from the material legacy of Pio provides part of the answer to the problem of their attitude towards the cult. But there is a socio-religious dimension to their perceptions alongside the material, institutional one. There is a clear distinction between the Sangiovannesi and devotees proper in respect of the cult, underlying which is an implicit dispute about the 'true message' of Pio.

Sangiovannesi and devotees are best compared by considering those townspeople who do often worship at the friary church. These may be especially devoted to Pio, but even they dissociate themselves from the 'fanatics', outsider devotees marked by their extreme, fanatical devotion. In the literature, these latter are frequently described as hysterical, disturbed women who, it is implied, embarrassed Pio and brought his cult into disrepute with their unseemly behaviour. In the eyes of the Sangiovannesi, the fanatics are above all outsiders who moved to the town under the pretext of devotion but who really came for another reason – sent away by their families for some sin, for example, or to open a boarding house. They spend their time in church, and in criticizing those who do not do likewise. They are like the local *sbizocc'ne*, any overly pious but hypocritical woman, except that the object of their devotion is Pio. Such devotees are sometimes described as '*i pacc'*', 'the crazy', or as 'the mad of the Cappuccini area'.[15] Clearly, normal respect for Pio as a man of God is one thing; exaggerated or mad behaviour is quite another matter.

Many pilgrims to San Giovanni Rotondo belong to a 'Padre Pio Prayer Group'. These groups were organized during Pio's lifetime (though not without controversy) to pray for his intentions and to support his charitable work. It is worth noting that no such prayer group exists in the town itself.

When I asked one of the town's priests (not a Capuchin friar) the reason for this, he told me that it was because the Sangiovannesi are not fanatical in their love of Pio. Other informants gave a similar response. It is clear that, for the Sangiovannesi, love for Pio is possible without 'fanatical' behaviour.

THE SACRED TRANSFORMED

In order to sharpen the distinction between townspeople and devotees, it is necessary to consider the shrine itself, what it signifies, and how the area has been transformed since the development of the cult.

The area of the shrine is sacred territory because it is imbued with the memory and spirit of the saint. Everywhere there are physical reminders of him in the form of statues and images. The tomb in the crypt is the most sacred place of all, but many places associated with him are marked out for the faithful – the place where he received the stigmata, his cell, the confessional he used, or simply, 'Place where Padre Pio sat'. Pio's image is also said to reproduce itself, in the wood grain of the confessional, on the pattern of the marble floor, and on a piece of rocky terrain about to be cleared behind the shrine.

The imagination of the pilgrim is well stimulated even before he or she makes the journey to the shrine. Pilgrims are usually familiar with the essential details of the life-story of their saint, namely that for most of his life he bore the wounds of Christ's crucifixion on his body, that he suffered physically, that he was mistreated and misunderstood by the church authorities, and that through him many miracles were and still are performed. The pilgrim's journey to San Giovanni Rotondo is, then, a classic journey to 'the centre'. That Pio bore the stigmata, like St Francis before him and like Christ himself, transforms the mountain of the Gargano into Mount Alverna (where Francis received the stigmata) but also, more importantly, into Calvary.

Themes of suffering and redemption are prominent in Pio's own perception of himself and his mission, and these themes are played out in the promotion of the cult, in the process by which 'the message' of Pio is interpreted. Pio is seen as Christ re-crucified, in a manner perhaps more urgent and vivid than St Francis. Devotees recall that Pio himself is quoted as saying, 'Everything Jesus suffered in the Passion, I suffer too' (Castello 1981: 165). Pio's living crucifixion was confirmed by other phenomena witnessed by pilgrims and devotees. Thus, one devotee told me of how she had had a vision of Pio wearing a crown of thorns; another witnessed the crucifixion of Christ taking place on the altar throughout Pio's mass. And on display in the shrine are items of clothing bearing bloodstains from the mystical flagellation of the saint.

Devotees who lived in the area of the shrine during Pio's lifetime stayed on after his death because they wanted to live where 'his spirit is strongest'. In their daily lives, focused around the shrine, they, like the pilgrims, encounter at every turn the sacred evoked by Pio.

For others who live in the town, however, that quality of the palpable sacred is not easily maintained. While it is true that many Sangiovannesi entertain a sense of wonder about Pio, they also often remark that they never noticed anything extraordinary about him. He had the stigmata, of course, but in other respects he appeared quite normal. 'I myself never saw any miracles', they told me. For them, the Cappuccini remains a different world, but it is a world which has been transformed by history. Once, it was clearly a sacred zone because it was the place of the hermits who possessed a miraculous image of the Madonna.[16] Now, this sacredness has been compromised. It has become a place of tourism, and a place of work for those employed in the hotels and in the hospital. It is a world that has been appropriated by various kinds of outsiders. The purely sacred has been brought closer to them in material and historical terms, yet in the process a new distance has been created, formed in part by their alienation from the material legacy of Pio and by the association of his culting with fanatical outsiders.

For the Sangiovannesi, the Cappuccini is at once the suburb of the rich (outsiders, businessmen, and doctors), the suburb of the hospital, the suburb of the shrine, and the suburb of the devotees, referred to as *i pacc'*. It is a zone of secular power, of sacred power, of worldly success, and of worldly failure. Its value as a local shrine has been undermined by the transformation and complication of its sacred nature.

THE 'TRUE MESSAGE' OF PIO

The problem I wished to address was this: why do the Sangiovannesi tend to dissociate themselves from 'everything that goes on up on the hill', even though they clearly regard Padre Pio as their patron saint and as one marked out by God? Why do they say that it has nothing to do with them, even though they recognize that the local economy is based on religious tourism and on the Casa Sollievo della Sofferenza?

For the Sangiovannesi, Padre Pio is a man who came from the outside to live in their town. He demonstrated his affection for them and their town through his concern for their material well-being. He founded the hospital because he saw their need. He also established nursery schools and schools for the handicapped, and started workers' co-operatives. He spoke on their behalf to people in power. Wealth was created, and new roads opened up the area to the outside world.

The Sangiovannesi thus recognize that Pio had a profound material effect on the life and development of their town. Nor is this recognition blunted by their perception of the subsequent appropriation of the material and spiritual legacy of the saint, their feeling that they have been excluded from the wealth that has been created and their view that the cult has been appropriated by fanatical misfits. Pio remains for them a man who entered *their* historical time and space and acted upon these to transform them. Some acknowledge his ability to work miracles, and regard him as a man marked out by the divine. Most lay stress, however, not on the cosmological significance of his spirituality, but on his humanity. All agree that Pio's greatest miracle was an economic one, namely the construction of the Casa Sollievo della Sofferenza.

By contrast, the pilgrim journeys from the outside to a place regarded as sacred by virtue of the holy person who lived and died there and whose spirit is felt to be still present in the place. This quality of the sacred is also created by the fact that the shrine is outside the pilgrim's mundane world. The pilgrim thus leaves the everyday world in which the sacred is encountered piecemeal and partially, to enter a world where historical time and space yield in significance to sacred time and space. Pio's shrine is important because it leads one out of the mundane into contact with the divine. This is the place where Pio was signed with the marks of the crucifixion and where he became, with Christ, a co-redeemer of humanity. On this mountain of the Gargano, the sacrifice of Calvary was renewed. The shedding of his blood released miraculous powers. The divine became palpable: Christ, the Virgin, the saints, the angels, and the spirits of the dead all came to Pio in this place. Graces were bestowed on people: they were healed, converted, and comforted.

For a brief time, pilgrims dwell in this world of cosmological significance. They come to San Giovanni Rotondo expecting certain kinds of experience, an expectation that is based on their familiarity with the myth of Pio. Thus, they are not surprised when they experience one of the mysterious but well-attested perfumes of Pio. They come expecting a spiritual uplift; they come in the hope of receiving a particular grace, a physical cure, peace of mind, or material assistance. One or other of these is always granted because the pilgrimage facilitates intimate contact with the divine in the form of the special powers felt to reside in this sacred place. 'No one ever ascends this mountain in vain', pilgrims say, for the mountain is a pathway to the divine.

The resident devotees are *a fortiori* inhabitants of this cosmological time and space. They also originally came from the outside as pilgrims; now they attempt to live permanently, not in the historical time and space of the Sangiovannesi, but in the ritual time and space of the pilgrim. This they can do only by remaining as much as possible in the vicinity of the shrine, by eschewing the company of the Sangiovannese and other non-devotees of Pio, and by living lives that are clearly not social in the normal, moral sense.

Many of these devotees are persons whose social status has conduced to their becoming religious virtuosi. The typical resident devotee is thought by a Sangiovannese to be an unmarried woman, and this stereotype is not unwarranted. They do not generally have families or visible kinship networks. They do not reproduce, nor do they seem to produce. They tend to live on pensions or private incomes, however small, or to work for the friars or the Casa Sollievo in the promotion of Pio, or they might run boarding houses. They do not work in the same way that the Sangiovannesi work. Indeed, they would say that their real work is the salvation of their souls and praying for the salvation of others.

Resident devotees typically express a loathing for the town and its residents. This attitude can be explained in part by their attempt to live their lives entirely in the sacred realm. They often comment that the Sangiovannesi never come to Pio's tomb, and have largely ignored his message. They are reluctant to leave the shrine area even to travel two kilometres down the hill into the town centre. Shopping trips, for example, are necessary but regrettable exits from the realm of the sacred, and are fraught with danger. The spirit of Pio is less tangible to them once they leave the Cappuccini zone. More importantly, leaving the sacred realm is likely to bring them into contact with malevolent forces – Satan and other evil spirits. Some devotees even feel that evil spirits operate through the Sangiovannesi themselves, who treat them badly, try to cheat them in commercial dealings, and so on. Living in San Giovanni Rotondo they describe as paradise on earth because of the presence of Pio. But it is also purgatory – a place where penance has to be done, often in the form of hazardous dealings with the outside world on their doorstep.

In the eyes of the Sangiovannesi, the resident devotees are outsiders in a double sense. They are literally from other parts of Italy, but they also inhabit a world which is not their own. They are fanatical in their devotion to Padre Pio. They see miracles in the most commonplace coincidences. They are obsessed with the idea of evil, both as moral failing and as diabolical incarnations. It becomes easy to see why such people are frequently referred to as crazy. Their self-claimed status as devotee is not recognized as a characteristic which pertains to the sacred, for their form of religiosity seems exaggerated. It is not regarded by the Sangiovannesi as valid or healthy, and is therefore described in secular terms. These people, it is implied, are not holy but unwell. In their fanaticism, they distort and devalue the message of Pio.

The lives of the devotees are thus the inverse of the lives of the townspeople. The world of the devotees is one in which the myths of Christianity, including that of Pio, are daily recreated through ritual, and through cautious avoidance of the world outside the shrine where historical time and place predominate and where the cosmological pales. The Sangiovannesi, for their part, inhabit this historical, secular world, in which Pio himself was intimately involved during his lifetime, and on which he made a considerable impact. There are, in effect, two Padre Pios, one cosmological, the other historical, one recognized by the devotees, the other by the Sangiovannesi; and just as the two images of this complex figure are mutually incompatible, so the respective groups espousing them are irreconcilable.

CONCLUSION

Analytically, a distinction could be made between resident devotees and pilgrims. From my perspective, however, this distinction is merely quantitative: the pilgrim enters cosmological time and space for a brief period only, whereas the resident devotee attempts to live permanently in that realm. The salient divide is between devotees – both resident and non-resident – on the one hand and the Sangiovannesi on the other. From the point of view of the townspeople, all devotees are – potentially, at least – fanatics. They all have a distorted view of the world, giving an exaggerated priority to the mythological and the cosmological at the expense of the material and the historical. For the Sangiovannesi, Pio's life has an historical importance measured primarily by the material changes which he wrought for their town. They cannot give priority to Pio's cosmological significance, since to do so would require participation in the ritual journey of the pilgrim, or leading the ascetic and asocial life of the resident devotee. For devotees, both resident and pilgrim, the shrine is sacred since it holds the promise of life to be transformed. For the Sangiovannesi, the shrine also has the quality of the sacred, but because it is symbolic of life already transformed.

Far from being a harmonious *axis mundi*, then, the shrine of Padre Pio is a place fraught with conflicting discourses, intense competition for control of wealth and resources, and contrasting interpretations of that aspect of the divine which has made its presence felt on earth. Given the brevity of their stay, it is unlikely that visiting pilgrims are aware of the struggles through which the sacred quality of the place is created, maintained, and disputed. Much less are they likely to appreciate that they, too, are part of this process. In responding to the call of those who promulgate the message of Pio, they contribute by their journey to the creation of the sacred aura which surrounds San Giovanni Rotondo. However, theirs is but one understanding, one discourse among the several which make up the divided, discordant whole.

NOTES

1 There are, of course, some notable exceptions. Finucane (1977), for example, considers specifically the changing geographical pattern of the attraction of the saint, cult, and shrine. Scarvaglieri conducted a sociological study of the religious lives of the people of Assisi and found that a hypothesized secularization was not proven, given 'the very persistence of Assisi as a shrine town, the centrality of religion and its being at the centre of the lives of the people of Assisi' (1980: 243–4). Fuller (1984), Parry (1980, 1982), Zeitlyn (1986) and Van der Veer (1988) examine pilgrimage to various Indian shrines, focusing on the shrines themselves and on the religious specialists who derive their living from them. See also the chapters by Eade and Bowman in this volume.

2 I carried out fieldwork in San Giovanni Rotondo from February 1986 to March 1987, and was supported by grants from the Commonwealth Scholarship Fund and the Central Research Fund of the University of London.

3 Scarvaglieri's study (1987), published after the completion of my research, gives a sociological account of the experience of pilgrims to San Giovanni Rotondo. The study is based largely on interviews and on the results of two questionnaires, one distributed to pilgrims at the shrine.

4 I refer to Pio as a saint, although he has not been officially canonized. The cause for his beatification was opened in 1983.

5 Resident outsiders also include those who have moved to the town for reasons of employment rather than because of devotion to Pio, but this group falls outside the scope of this chapter.

6 There are three quite separate Franciscan orders for men. The Capuchins were initiated as a reform movement in 1525 by a group of friars who wished to re-establish the original austerity of the Rule of St Francis, and who wished to live an eremitical life.

7 The town and the friary precincts are no longer physically separate, as will be discussed later.

8 See Acquaviva and Eisermann (1982: 25–68) for the indicators of the 'under-development' of the Gargano in the early part of this century.

9 Saldutto (1986) records that the first newspaper article about Pio appeared in a Roman daily *Il Giornale d'Italia*, 9 May 1919.

10 Of note is the fact that among the many influential benefactors was Barbara Ward. At that time a journalist with *The Economist*, a British weekly journal, she visited Pio in 1947 and later convinced her fiancé Robert Jackson that UNRRA, for whom he worked, should support the Casa Sollievo.

11 This is dealt with at length in McKevitt (1988).

12 Indeed, an Italian academic once told me that he had visited the shrine of Padre Pio but insisted that he had not seen any town to speak of.

13 These figures date from the period of my fieldwork, 1986–87.

14 Indeed, devotees often state: 'Padre Pio said, "I belong to everyone".'

15 D'Apolito, a Sangiovannesi confrère of Padre Pio, writes: 'One day some confrères and I, in speaking with Padre Pio about some fanatical and hot-headed people who came from every part of Italy to San Giovanni Rotondo, showing signs of mental derangement and madness, pointed out that they disturbed the peace and serenity of the shrine and that they should be taken to sanatoria. Joking and witty, Padre Pio replied: "There should be a great fence around this area and a sign: Lunatic Asylum"' (1981: 245).

16 In those days, it was a local shrine of the kind described by Christian (1972) in northern Spain.

REFERENCES

Acquaviva, S. and Eisermann, G. (1982) *La Montagna del Sole*, Torino: ERI.

Alessandro da Ripabottoni (1983) *Padre Pio: Il Cireneo di Tutti*, San Giovanni Rotondo: Edizioni Padre Pio da Pietrelcina.

Castello, N. (1981) *Padre Pio Teaches Us*, San Giovanni Rotondo: Edizioni Casa Sollievo della Sofferenza.

Christian, W. A. (1972) *Person and God in a Spanish Valley*, New York: Seminar Press.

D'Apolito, A. (1981) *Padre Pio of Pietrelcina: Memories, Experiences, Testimonials*, San Giovanni Rotondo: Edizioni Padre Pio da Pietrelcina.

Eliade, M. (1959) *The Sacred and the Profane*, New York: Harcourt Brace Jovanovich.

Finucane, R. A. (1977) *Miracles and Popular Beliefs in Medieval England*, Oxford: Oxford University Press.

Fuller, C. J. (1984) *Servants of the Goddess*, Cambridge: Cambridge University Press.

McKevitt, C. (1988) 'Suffering and sanctity: an anthropological study of a saint cult in a southern Italian town', unpublished Ph.D. thesis, London School of Economics, University of London.

Morinis, E. A. (1984) *Pilgrimage in the Hindu Tradition: A Case Study of West Bengal*, Delhi: Oxford University Press.

Pagnossin, G. (1978) *Il Calvario di Padre Pio*, Padova.

Parry, J. P. (1980) 'Ghosts, greed and sin: the occupational identity of the Benares funeral priests', *Man* 15: 88–111.

_____ (1982) 'Sacrificial death and the necrophagous ascetic', in M. Bloch and J. P. Parry (eds) *Death and the Regeneration of Life*, Cambridge: Cambridge University Press.

Pio da Pietrelcina (1980) *Letters. Volume 1*, ed. Gerardo di Flumeri, San Giovanni Rotondo: Edizioni Padre Pio da Pietrelcina.

Saldutto, G. (1986) *Un Tormentato Settennio nella Vita di Padre Pio da Pietrelcina*, San Giovanni Rotondo: Edizioni Padre Pio da Pietrelcina.

Sallnow, M. J. (1987) *Pilgrims of the Andes: Regional Cults in Cusco*, Washington, DC: Smithsonian Institution Press.

Scarvaglieri, G. (1980) *La Vita Religiosa degli Assisani*, Padova: Edizioni Messagero.

_____ (1987) *Pellegrinaggio ed Esperienza Religiosa: Ricerca Socio-Religiosa sul Santuario Santa Maria della Grazie*, San Giovanni Rotondo: Edizioni Padre Pio da Pietrelcina.

Turner, V. W. and Turner, E. (1978) *Image and Pilgrimage in Christian Culture: Anthropological Perspectives*, Oxford: Basil Blackwell.

Van der Veer, P. (1988) *Gods on Earth: The Management of Religious Experience and Identity in a North Indian Pilgrimage Centre*, London: Athlone Press.

Zeitlyn, S. (1986) 'Sacrifice and the sacred in a Hindu tirtha: the case of Pushkar India', unpublished Ph.D. thesis, London School of Economics, University of London.

Chapter four

Christian ideology and the image of a holy land
The place of Jerusalem pilgrimage in the various Christianities

Glenn Bowman

INTRODUCTION

The great majority of the world's holy cities and sacred shrines attract pilgrims from culturally circumscribed catchment areas, and thus host pilgrims united by strong degrees of cultural homogeneity. Jerusalem, on the other hand, draws pilgrims from a vast multitude of nations and cultural traditions. During religious festivals, which tend to be imbricated because of the antagonistic engagement of Judaism, Christianity, and Islam, Jerusalem's streets swarm with men and women displaying a rainbow of secular and religious costumes, speaking a cacophony of languages, and pursuing a plethora of divine figures. Other sacred centres which attract pilgrims from areas as heterogeneous as those which provide Jerusalem's pilgrims – eminent among these being Mecca, which none the less services only the sects of a single religion – funnel their devotees through ritual routines which mask differences beneath identical repertoires of movement and utterance. Jerusalem's pilgrims, on the other hand, go to different places at different times where they engage in very different forms of worship. The result is a continuous crossing and diverging – often marked by clashes – of bodies, voices, and religious artefacts. Jerusalem does not, in fact, appear so much as *a* holy city but as a *multitude* of holy cities – as many as are the religious communities which worship at the site – built over the same spot, operating at the same moment, and contending for hegemony.

This synchronicity of Jewish, Muslim, and Christian holy cities suggests that what makes the city holy to the various groups which 'go up' to Jerusalem is not something found in the city but, instead, something brought from outside and matched up there with monuments to, and markers of, sacredness. The various Jerusalems function as signs in the diverse discourses on religion, power, and identity of the visiting groups.

Just as those discourses are created by the pilgrims' home cultures, so too do these signs render meaning from, and direct it back towards, the cultures which mobilize them. Each Jerusalem experienced by each group rises less from the walls and streets of the literal city than from images of the holy city and its environs imbibed in distant places while the pilgrims-to-be listened to stories and songs, engaged in religious ceremonies, observed sacred and secular art works, and read pilgrims' tales and travellers' narratives. The holy city is, in other words, a place where pilgrims who have inherited or developed certain images of a 'Jerusalem' during enculturation elsewhere can embody those images and engage them as aspects of the material world.

The study which follows will examine the processes and problems involved in reifying the imaginary as these relate to the construction of holy sites, the organization of rituals, and the interaction of groups with different imaginings of Jerusalem. My account will concentrate on Christian pilgrimage, as this was the subject of my fieldwork in Jerusalem and the so-called 'Holy Land' between 1983 and 1985 and during shorter visits in 1987 and 1988. Such a circumscription of my topic will serve to amplify, rather than to mute, my assertion about the problems of rooting a rich diversity of meanings in a single terrain. It will expose the number of diverse and mutually contradictory ways persons nominally united within a single religious tradition approach a place which they share not only with each other but also with the devotees of two other world religions.

IMAGE AND TEXT

To understand the sources of discord among the several Christian experiences of Jerusalem and the Holy Land we must be aware of the 'textuality' of Christian imaginings of the places. The adoption of the Judaic Old Testament by Christianity substantially transformed the field of reference of that text. For Jews, the Old Testament is typically read as a chronicle of God's intervention in their national history, which includes within it numerous divine promises of the nation's future, in-worldly realization of a God-granted destiny. Diasporic Christianity, in separating that text from the history of the Jewish nation and supplementing it with chronicles of and prophecies related to the life of Jesus, transformed 'that mixture of folklore, ethical exhortation and nationalist political propaganda' (Kamenka 1973: 4) into a referential system which, no longer bound to a particular people or to a particular historical movement, could be assimilated into other discourses and other historical movements. The Bible, while retaining its status as a record of God's actions in and statements to the world, became the charter myth of numerous groups and institutions which mobilized its stories and its prophecies to suit strategies and contexts not only radically different from those of the Palestinian Jews but also, in time, disparate from those of other groups which legitimated their activities and their world views in biblical terms.

The Bible may have been the central text on which Christians based their identities and in terms of which they legitimated their activities, but Christians from different cultural milieux constructed in the midst of different historical processes would in fact be reading their lives and their surroundings in terms of very different myths while nominally celebrating the same record of God and the world. The centrality of that text meant that it was the reference point by which religious Christians judged the world through which they moved, but the proliferation of meanings accreted around it, as it variously developed through the historical spread of the Christian faith, meant that the worlds constituted in its terms were very different – even when, as in the case of Holy Land pilgrimages, those worlds were nominally the same.

This is not, however, to say that the Bible is, in Barthes' terms, a completely 'writerly' text (Barthes 1975). Christianity as it developed evolved a substantial, and authoritarian, institutional framework which strove to restrain 'semantic drift', establish doctrine, and extirpate heterodoxy. None the less, the spread of the Christian faith through numerous cultures and environments and the necessity for that faith – if it were to remain convincing – to give meaning to the lives of individuals within those different settings mean that there has always been a strong centrifugal impulse operating within the religion. As long as that drive towards difference is constrained within a single institutional framework it generates relatively insignificant variations in regional practices, but when the framework itself disintegrates – as it has numerous times throughout the past two millennia (Frend 1984; Herrin 1987) – new institutions develop to maintain difference and foster further variation. Before passing on to a consideration of how various western Christianities enact their versions of Christianity in the Holy Land, I would like to discuss briefly the substantial differences between the epistemologies and soteriologies of three major strains of the religion: Orthodoxy, Catholicism, and Protestantism.

All three branches of Christianity have inherited from their Judaic forebears an interpretation of the world which poses a dialectical relationship between the unfavourable state of the sphere in which people live and a redeemed domain, at present unattainable, into which people will, through the grace of God, eventually enter. In Judaic terms this other world is to be realized in history and will offer the nation of Israel redemption from its history of misfortune and oppression. Early Christianity, by defining inclusion within the church as a matter of election rather than of membership within a territorial or kinship group, radically transformed the Judaic relationship between the land, the people, and history. Christianity asserted that salvation was attainable only through the forging of a personal bond with God, thus moving the emphasis of the salvatory process from a collectivity defined in terms of blood and national identity to the individual. This, according to Dumont (1982), elevates the individual's personal relation to God to a supreme value while simultaneously devaluing his or her involvement with the secular world and its institutions.

Despite a radical shift of emphasis away from the nation in history towards the individual in eternity, Christianity, in all subsequent incarnations, maintained the concept of a collective organization into which believers entered through baptism which, like Noah's Ark, would serve to carry those given God's grace out of danger and into redemption. This institution was the church, which defined itself as the 'New Israel'. Within the parameters of the inherited biblical tradition there was considerable room for diversity, and the historical development of Christianity played numerous variations on the themes of the redeemed world, the individual desirous of entry into it, and the nature of the church which would offer access.

Christianity, as Gibbon (1914) and his many successors have pointed out, became the religion of an imperial system well on its way to fragmentation. Whether or not Gibbon is correct in his assertion that Christianity actually contributed to the decline and fall of the Roman Empire cannot concern us here, but it is significant that as Constantine adopted Christianity as his personal religion and extended to it the support that would assist it in its rise to hegemony, he was in the process of shifting the imperial capital from Rome to Constantinople. The transfer acknowledged that the centre of the empire, as a socio-economic entity, had effectively already been displaced from the west to the east, and that the west, threatened by barbarian invasion and political anarchy, was no longer as governable or as economically viable as the eastern sectors of the empire (Anderson 1974). Christianity was widespread and influential throughout both sectors of the empire, but the different conditions under which it would evolve in the two domains resulted in very different articulations of the nature of mankind, the world, and the possibilities of salvation.

The dualism between this world and a redeemed world fundamental to Christian epistemology allows for the possibility, developed fully in eastern Christianity, that the state can be left to deal with issues pertaining to the fallen world while the church concerns itself with matters related to humanity's escape from this world and into the next. People can 'render unto Caesar that which is Caesar's' so long as Caesar is willing to allow them to 'render unto God that which is God's'. In the Byzantine east, where a Christian emperor granted the Christian church full spiritual authority while dealing efficiently with secular matters, this division of labour could be maintained. In the west, on the contrary, the state was not able to maintain the order that the church needed if it were to deal with people's spiritual needs. The collapse of urban infrastructures, the threat of barbarian invasions, and the frequency and violence of peasant revolts, such as those of the Bacaudae and Circumcelliones, led the western church in the fourth and fifth centuries to take over, in effect, the functions of the faltering state.

The Latin church developed its political programme and its theology in this situation, surrounded by ample evidence that the existing state apparatus could not only not defend its citizens but was actually, through exploitation, indifference, and expropriation, inflicting degradation and destruction upon them. Western theology, as articulated by Ambrose and Augustine amongst others, argued that it was the church's duty to ensure that divine grace, provided through the agency of the church, would be available to people in the world. The church was, therefore, responsible for imposing an order on the temporal world which would allow people access to that grace. The medieval theory of kingship, which Herrin sees as having been prepared in the late classical west, was based not on the concept of rendering unto Caesar what was Caesar's but on the idea that the church would work politically and theologically to impel Caesar to use his goods and his powers to expand and maintain Catholic hegemony. Central to this western development was what Dumont calls 'the papal assumption of a political function... [whereby] the spiritual is conceived as superior to the temporal *on the temporal level itself*, as if it was a superior degree of the temporal' (Dumont 1982: 16–17, emphasis in original). This shift of emphasis whereby, instead of seeing the temporal world as something to transcend through religious devotion, Latin Christians consecrate the political realm by forcing it to 'participate in absolute, universalist values' (ibid: 17) makes for substantial differences between Orthodox and Latin interpretations of the proper life of a person in the world and the appropriate role of the *sacra* in that life.

Lay Orthodox Christians see life as divided into two stages: a period which stretches from childhood until the moment one's own children are married off during which one is deeply involved in social life through the establishment, raising, and supporting of a family; and a phase during which one sheds social and familial responsibilities and turns one's attention to sacred things in preparation for ascension after death into Paradise (Hirschon 1989: 225–32). One's behaviour during the earlier, material, phase of life does not, except when one breaks communion with God, determine whether or not one will, after death, ascend to Paradise; lay Orthodox theology assumes that the sins of the world are the results of living in a fallen world and that they will be punished in that world and not in an afterlife (Campbell 1964: 323–6). The separation of the fallen and the redeemed worlds, which is a consequence of Adam's and Eve's sin of devotion to the world rather than to its creator, is in large part complete, with only the bridges of the *sacra* – those things, like icons or liturgies, which co-exist in both worlds – to bring them into contact.

What is important in Orthodox theology is that the Christian, as he or she approaches the moment when death will provide escape from this world, establishes full communion with God so that he or she can become dedicated to God himself and throw off involvement with the illusion of a world that seems to exist apart from its creator. As Campbell was told by the Sarakatsanos villagers with whom he worked in northern Greece, humans are, because of their enmeshment in a mortal world, subject to envy and sensuality – 'conditions which imply an attachment to material things which leads man away from God' (ibid: 326). The extirpation of these 'ancestral sins' through devotion to those things – holy persons, icons, and liturgies – through which God reveals that he, and he alone, creates and gives meaning to existence, enables the Orthodox to enter into the Paradise which God has opened to all those who recognize its existence.

In Latin Christianity, salvation is much more problematic. The fact that the world itself becomes a domain for God-directed activity elides the border between the fallen world and the redeemed world which, in Orthodoxy, is so carefully drawn. Whereas in the Orthodox world the church functions to make manifest in the life of mortals the traces of the immortality towards which they should strive as they begin to shuck off involvement in the secular world, the Latin churches serve to direct people as to how they should pursue their lives within the fallen world so as to earn Paradise after death. In consequence, one's chances of salvation are interpreted in terms of the degree to which one has done God's work during one's life.

This expansion of the domain of sacred activity has significant consequences for Latin theories of salvation. In Orthodoxy, the redemption brought about by Christ's intervention in history is cosmological and hence eventually universal. In Latin theology, however, salvation is granted only to those who have fully accorded their actions and thoughts with a world-historical will made manifest by an institution – the church – established within and operating on the secular world. This implies, first of all, that there is a substantial element of wastage (the damned) within Latin soteriology; only a very small percentage of humankind will prove itself worthy of attaining Paradise. Furthermore, divine grace flows only through the church and can operate only on those obedient to the will of God as interpreted by the church. Consequently, that institution – if it is to do the work of God in bringing all those worthy of salvation to redemption – must increase its membership to include the entirety of those in the world capable of earning redemption. It must, furthermore, direct those within its purview as to how to live so as to please God. Brown (1964), Frend (1971), Asad (1983: 242–5), and others have examined the role granted to coercion (in missionization, conversion, establishing orthodoxy, enforcing obedience, and waging holy war) by an institution which defines itself as the sole organ of the only significant values operative in the world, but I am more concerned here with the pedagogical function of the church as an institution which makes evident to its members how they should act to please God and earn salvation.

Whereas the *sacra* in Orthodoxy serves to disengage believers from the false values of a fallen world in preparation for their admission into the redeemed world, the religious in Latin theology serves instead to impose a particular ethics on activity in that fallen world itself. Within Orthodoxy the divine liturgy as well as other vehicles of the sacred like icons or holy relics serve as means for allowing people to 'step out' of illusion and to see creation, as a whole, in relation to its creator. Orthodox believers, in Greece as well as in the Holy Land, have several times told me that when they stand within an Orthodox church, its walls and iconostasis dense with icons and its ceilings painted with stars and pictures of the Pantocrator, they stand in Paradise in the presence of God, the Virgin Mary, and all the saints. Their entry into holy space presages their entry, at death, into eternity.

In the Latin churches, on the other hand, knowledge of the sacred is always mobilized back towards activity in the world. The liturgy makes clear to believers the debt owed to their God who took human form and, in that form, was humiliated and judicially murdered so as to grant humankind the possibility of salvation. The structure of the sermons and of the devotions is designed to inspire worshippers with faith in the power of God and with models for behaving in the world in accordance with that power. Each week, and for the particularly devout each day, is dedicated to a particular saint or holy incident which provides a particular lesson on how to live one's life. Religious art, instead of – like the icon – providing 'a patch of clear visibility' (Brown and MacCormack 1982: 212) through which the devotee can see into Paradise, is purely educational: it provides models for meditation which, rather than offering the meditator momentary access into the redeemed world, teach him or her the sorts of activities that God rewards. The lessons are inspirational and meant to provoke the devotee into action in the world. Thus, unlike in Orthodoxy where one engages the sacred precisely to the degree that one's age or gender enables one to disengage from the secular, in the Latin churches men and women are expected to model their behaviour throughout the whole of their lives according to the lessons of the church. Latin devotion, to use Dumont's terminology, is much more 'in-worldly' than is that of Orthodoxy (Dumont 1982).

The great heterodoxy of Latin Christianity, spanning as it does numerous manifestations of Catholicism as well as a bewildering diversity of Protestant sects, might lead the reader to doubt whether one can talk of a 'Latin ontology'. It is, however, precisely the in-worldliness of the Latin perspective which unites those churches, and a consequence of that in-worldliness that gives them their apparent diversity. The correlate of the church's sanctification of the world as a domain of religious action is a secularization of the church as a worldly institution. Ullmann (1970), in pointing out that the history of western theology made the church the sole legislator of reality, also indicates the sources of an élitism which alienated the greater part of its members from the benefits it promised: the priests alone are functionally qualified to govern the Christian body. This political élitism joined with the spiritual élitism implicit in the Augustinian concept of the *massa peccati* to provoke a *de facto* refusal by the church to include its lay members in the practices designed to offer them the chance of salvation. Dix points out that 'in the West holy communion became practically a clerical and monastic monopoly after the fifth century' (1945: 598) and that 'with the increased emphasis on "consecration" (the "liturgy" of the celebrant alone) there went a parallel movement by which the layman lost all active participation in the rest of the rite, the offertory and the communion – his "liturgy". He became a mere spectator and listener' (ibid). The lay population was thus subordinated to the secular rule of the church without access to the spiritual grace which the church claimed legitimated that rule. This exclusion was to lead, in the Middle Ages, to several suppressed popular heretical movements which were, in effect, social revolutions against the hegemony of the church. Subsequently, however, the more general spread of literacy and lay power in the late medieval period initiated a theological assault on the legitimacy of the church. Wycliffe, Huss, and subsequent fundamentalists argued that the Bible was the sole criterion of doctrine and that it provided no sanction for the immense and corrupt power of the Latin church. The mediation of the church as the sole vehicle of salvation existing between God and mankind was thrown into question and the Bible was given priority as the Word of God present in the world.

This, as I have suggested above, was not a solution to the problem of understanding the divine will but merely the initiation of several new discourses on God, humankind, and moral activity. By throwing aside the authority of the Roman church, the Protestant reformers once again released the biblical text from the constraints of tradition so that it could speak new words to new contexts. The various answers which would be thrown up by the multiple Protestant sects over the next five hundred years to questions of 'who is worthy of redemption?', 'what is the relationship of the sect to the world?', and 'how is God to continue to make his will manifest in the world?' are too diverse to examine here. It is worth stressing, however, the ontological continuity which survives Protestant-ism's rupturing of Catholic hegemony. Protestantism, like Catholicism, presents a discourse on transforming the world in accordance with a transcendental will. It retains the idea of an elect which works that will and of others, outside grace, who neither assist God nor will benefit from redemption. Divine will is still seen to be channelled through a com-munity, more or less institutionalized in the world, which serves to interpret and articulate it and, in some cases, to impose it by force on those who do not submit to it willingly. The individual still gains, or loses, salvation in relation to how he or she accords his or her life in the world to models ordained as God-given. The chief difference is that the Protes-tant sects draw more directly on biblical texts than on the authority of an interpretative institution for their models of devotion.

THE PRACTICE OF PILGRIMAGE

In examining the ways groups within these various traditions impose their models of devotion on the Holy Land one must remain aware that pilgrimage, in the Christian tradition, is voluntaristic. Holy Land pilgrimage is popular because it allows pilgrims to meditate away from the cares and distractions of their everyday lives on places and moments central to their sense of themselves as Christians. Holy Land pilgrimage may, in the pilgrims' experience, amplify the religious impulse, but it does not change the signal; it is an aid to devotion rather than a necessary part of it. Even when Catholicism offered indulgences linked to the holy places or instituted penitential pilgrimages to those places, these were not linked to a conception of the holy places as being, in any epistemological sense, different from the places from which pilgrims departed. The development of the system of indulgences was, as its subsequent extension to most holy places within Christendom has shown, meant to ensure the maintenance of a Catholic presence in those places (Lea 1896; Watkins 1920) while penitential pilgrimages served to disengage serious transgressors from the sites of their transgressions for substantial periods of time (Berlière 1890; Vogel 1964); it was worldly logistics and not any sense of the singularity of the Holy Land which motivated these practices. This explains why, in contradistinction to, say, Islamic pilgrimage to Mecca, devotional practices in the Holy Land do not differ in any substantial way from those the pilgrims engage in in their originary milieu. This continuity of practice has given rise to a long theological controversy on the worth of pilgrimage in which opposition to the popular practice has been grounded on the assertion that one is no more likely to find God in a pilgrimage centre than in any other sanctified place and that, in fact, the distractions of the journey are more likely to carry one away from God and the holy life than towards them (Constable 1976).

In what follows, I will examine the pilgrimage practices of three groups of Christian pilgrims in order to show the way that those practices, all acted out in Jerusalem and its environs, are differentially structured by the ontologies of their particular sectarian alliances. I have chosen these three out of the twenty-seven Christian communities which regularly promote pilgrimages to the Holy Land because I have travelled with and observed them and because they seem somehow particularly suited to display the range of pilgrim practices enacted there.

The first group was made up of forty-eight Greek Orthodox Cypriots brought together from a wide area of villages and towns by a pilgrimage organizer with ties to the Jerusalem Brotherhood of the Holy Sepulchre. One group of nine men and women within the larger group came from a single village and was accompanied by its parish priest, but the guide for the group as a whole was an archimandrite, normally resident in Gaza, who came up to Jerusalem to assist with pilgrim groups during the period leading up to and including Holy Week. The second group I will discuss was a group of fifteen English and Irish Catholics who were members of a lay organization called the 'Little Way', dedicated to the performance of acts of charity and devotion in accordance with the model set by the life of Saint Thérèse of Lisieux. They had been brought together through an advertisement in the organization's journal and were guided by a Franciscan priest, Father Raphael. The final group, part of a massive crowd of 1600 Christian Zionists who had come to Israel to celebrate the Jewish Feast of Tabernacles, was made up of evangelical Protestants from the United States, South Africa, Great Britain, and Holland. The group was addressed in a large convention hall throughout the week it was in the country by various Israeli politicians and members of the so-called 'International Christian Embassy'. The few excursions its members made outside the hall were led by state-licensed Israeli guides.

While keeping in mind the reservations expressed by Clifford (1988) about the possibility of extrapolating general ethnological statements from encounters with particular individuals and small groups, I will none the less try to indicate the ways the particular pilgrimage practices of these groups coincided with general tendencies within Orthodox, Catholic, and Protestant pilgrimages. I must, however, assert that each group was distinctive in terms of its constituency, its background, and the particularities of its experiences and that, therefore, the three are not being presented as 'typical' representatives of the wider religious entities.

ORTHODOX PILGRIMAGE

Greek Orthodox pilgrims envision their pilgrimage to the holy places as a sloughing off of impurities consequent on the Fall in preparation for death and resurrection. They step out of a world in which they have been deeply involved in the sins consequent on mortality and into a world which has, with Christ's life and death, partaken in the process of turning mortal into immortal flesh. Traditionally, Greek and Cypriot pilgrims come to the Holy Land in old age to prepare themselves for a good death and for their subsequent assumption into the redeemed world promised by Jesus, and the composition of the group with which I travelled conformed with this pattern.

Orthodox pilgrimage is made up of two types of activity, although these are not necessarily arranged sequentially. The first involves the transformation of the fallen into the redeemed, while the second celebrates their consequent participation in Paradise itself. Within the first is enacted the process of the individual's own transfiguration, and pilgrims, before going on pilgrimage, prepare for this by confessing their sins. On entering the Holy Land, in order to mark the boundary between a world in which they have dedicated themselves to worldly concerns and one in which they will devote themselves to the eternal, the pilgrims have their feet washed by monks of the Brotherhood of the Holy Sepulchre who meet them at the harbours or airports. At some point during their pilgrimage they will be baptized in the River Jordan in order, like Christ himself, to have the Holy Spirit descend upon them.

The baptism at the Jordan is, for the pilgrims, a cathartic reunification with the divine image within them which has, through the years, been tarnished and covered over by the corruption consequent on their mortality. When, in 1984, Archimandrite Meliton, the Cypriot pilgrims, and I arrived at what, at present, passes as the River Jordan baptism site, the pilgrims tore off their clothing, dressed themselves in white funeral shrouds which they had bought in Jerusalem (some of which were imprinted with an icon of Christ's resurrection from the tomb), and plunged into the river. Meliton, singing an Orthodox hymn with the term *metamorphosis* (transfiguration) repeated throughout, splashed water on them with a sprig of thyme, and then went through the motions of rebaptizing them. Later, some rolled about in the water, splashing others gleefully, while many dipped bits of clothing – among other things the funeral shrouds of others who had been unable to come themselves but who, like the pilgrims, would be buried in these shrouds – in the river before storing them carefully away in plastic bags which they had been filling throughout the day with crosses, burnt candles, bits of flowers, and small flasks of lamp oil from other holy sites. Afterwards, on the bus, Archimandrite Meliton announced to all 'now that you have sloughed off your sinful bodies and have risen in the body of Christ you must love one another as brothers, must pray for the peace of all nations, must obey all God's commandments, and must live in his ways'. He then went on to say, that 'this does not mean you have left this world; you must not give up your duties, and that includes those to your wives and husbands' because, as he explained to me later, it was important 'to fight against the simple assumptions of their minds'.

The second aspect of Orthodox pilgrimage is collective participation in the eternity imaged in the places where Christ had worked his redemptive mission. For the Greek pilgrims, the Holy Land reminds them of the places which they commemorate in their churches and icons at home. Each place has, in history, played a specific part in manifesting the divine promise of deification to the world, and so too each place – as a bridge to the eternal – has a particular significance. However, individual sites, like particular icons, provide entry into the entirety of the redeemed world and, once that entry has been effected, there is no reason to consider any moment of eternity as different from any other. In Latin holy places, which instruct the pilgrim and then refer him or her back to the world, each site mobilizes the incident which has occurred in it to teach pilgrims specific lessons to be applied to their worldly lives. The particularity of Orthodox holy places, on the other hand, is discarded as soon as it has served to bring pilgrims out of the fallen world and into the risen world manifest within the icon-dense churches built over or next to the memorialized sites: an historical moment is only distinct from others in the light of temporality – in eternity all moments are the same.

I was bemused, while travelling with Orthodox pilgrims, to see that the guides always presented biblical and historical information about holy places before entering on to the property of those places, and that the pilgrims were so uninterested in those details that, as the pilgrimages proceeded, the guides took to keeping the pilgrims confined to the buses until they had finished their historico-biblical sketches. Once released, the pilgrims would rush impatiently into the churches and proceed around the interiors kissing all the icons without granting any – except perhaps those of Jesus and the Virgin Mary – particular attention. The interiors of churches prefigured Paradise, and, since all the saints in Paradise were present through their icons within the churches, there was no reason why a pilgrim should grant any of them, except perhaps the Lord and his mother who had effected their *metastoicheiosis*, or trans-elementation, any more attention than any other. Icons which figured forth the incidents that were supposed to have occurred on the site, and the actual remains of those places, received no more reverence than did the other icons, although some pilgrims would pay particular attention to the icons of the saints of their name days.

Perhaps the one thing that makes the Holy Land more sacred than the other *sacra* experienced in the life of a Greek Orthodox person is that it is the most realistic icon, or representation, of the spiritual truths expressed in all Orthodox religious forms. This 'realism' is not, however, simply manifest in the sites themselves. The fact that the places are supposed to be the same places through which Christ walked and around which he did his work does not appear to be universally appreciated. On the same pilgrimage one can see people who kiss every available rock and drink from every source of water and others who show enthusiasm only when they are inside churches revering and commenting on icons identical to those in their churches at home. Travels around the holy places are, for the Orthodox, a desirable but unnecessary supplement to their pilgrimage; what the pilgrimage to the Holy Land is about, at heart, is being present in Jerusalem during the holy feasts. It is during these festivals that the significant realism of the holy places comes into play, when Orthodox pilgrims, in the company of thousands of other Orthodox persons from throughout the Mediterranean basin, witness, for perhaps the only time in their lives, an image of the community of mankind united in Christ.

Campbell and Hirschon, in their examinations of religion in Greek community life, have both emphasized the fact that Orthodox existence is torn by a deeply felt contradiction whereby people recognize that they are one in Christ but are at the same time aware that, because of the curse of mortality, they live in a world where others are for the most part perceived as ruthless competitors for scarce resources. Campbell points out that it is only during Holy Week that the Sarakatsani transcend that isolation and see themselves, at least hypothetically, as part of the community to which Christ has granted them access:

> The idea of Christ's brotherhood implies, at least, the brotherhood of the Sarakatsani of Zagori, and, by extension (although less certainly), the brotherhood of Orthodox Greeks. Christ sacrificed Himself not for one but for all. Not the least miracle of Easter is the measure of social goodwill. There is an easy warmth of greeting and attitude between unrelated men which is entirely foreign to the tense aggressiveness that is the formal idiom of social life at other times.... The union of men in Christ is reflected at the level of social relations in an expression of ideal solidarity which for a moment breaks down the barriers which isolate family from family and community from community.
>
> (Campbell 1964: 350)

During Holy Week in Jerusalem, and to a lesser extent during the two other feasts for which Orthodox pilgrims come to the Holy City (the Feast of the Assumption of the Virgin, and that of the Exaltation of the Cross), Orthodox pilgrims are able to transcend that contradiction and see that ideal community bodied forth, as it were, in the flesh. For days the streets and churches are filled with elderly Greek pilgrims who are not, in any significant way, in competition with others and who, for perhaps the first time in their lives, are not in places scarred by memories of conflicts which have involved them. During the ceremonies that bring both the Lenten fast and the Holy Land pilgrimages to their fulfilment, all the pilgrims commemorate collectively the process of redemption they have mirrored individually or in smaller groups throughout their lives and their pilgrimage. They then engage together in the fruit of those processes. With Christ's resurrection the universal transformation of the fallen world is effected, and as that *anastasis* is celebrated in the Holy Sepulchre an image of mankind, united not in temporality but in eternity, is brought forth. At the Ceremony of the Holy Fire the experience of communitas reaches a peak as thousands of pilgrims, crammed to the point of immobility into the confines of the Anastasis, pass the Holy Fire – announcing the imminence of the resurrection – from hand to hand until the whole church is bright with the flames of thousands of 'resurrection candles'. Later in the evening, when the resurrection of Christ is announced and as the pilgrims prepare to break the Lenten Fast communally, they sing together the *Christos Anesti*:

> Christ is risen from the dead,
> trampling down death by death,
> and to those in the tomb
> he bestows life.

(translation Hirschon 1989: 242)

CATHOLIC PILGRIMAGE

Catholic pilgrimage, unlike its Orthodox counterpart, is not strictly regulated by a liturgical calendar, nor does the celebration of universal communality play the same role. Catholic groups come to the Holy Land throughout the year, and while many attend as individuals or in families the larger proportion come in groups active as organizations in the world outside. In large part Catholic pilgrimage is inspirational; although plenary indulgences are still given, priests and pilgrims alike spoke of them to me as atavisms. People come to the Holy Land to be renewed in their faith so that they can subsequently re-engage their ordinary lives with rejuvenated energy and a revived sense of purpose. A number of priests with whom I went around the holy places were members of the Maryknoll Brothers who had, after several years of missionary work in Bolivia, come to the Holy Land on a ten-week programme of spiritual revitalization. One

of them told me that the awareness of Christ that he had felt after travelling
through the places Jesus had walked and preached left him profoundly
inspired: 'I wish I had done this before I had entered my calling because
I would have been much more dedicated to the spirit and less non-
emotional and rationalistic.'

The idea that pilgrimage serves as a revitalization of spiritual energies
drained by involvement in the labours of the secular world makes Catholic
pilgrimage much more individuated than that of the Orthodox. Instead of
a cosmological celebration of the community of mankind in Christ, the
Catholics engage, as individuals or in groups bound by a shared purpose,
in a process of being repossessed by the power that gives meaning to their
personal lives and labours. This individuation releases Catholic pilgrimage from the timetable of communal feasts. Whereas in Orthodoxy the
holy places and the holy dates in the church calendar are moments at which
the temporal participates in the eternal, in Catholicism the sites and the
days are sources of inspiration which do not reach beyond the world but
point to the appropriateness of certain activities and attitudes in the world.
Their significance can be meditated upon at any time, and therefore even
those groups which attempt to structure their travels through the holy
places in accordance with the church calendar often do so on dates which
are not aligned with the calendar itself. A group of Catholics from
Montmartre in Paris, for example, organize an annual pilgrimage where
they move through the holy places according to an itinerary arranged to
reflect, in place, the annual cycle of liturgy. This pilgrimage takes place
in August and lasts for two weeks.

The Little Way pilgrims with whom I toured Jerusalem were lay donors
to the 'Little Way' charity, and had come to the Holy Land on a week's
pilgrimage (three weeks before Easter) in order 'to celebrate their common calling together'. Whenever possible they stayed in Carmelite
guesthouses (like those in Nazareth and on Mt Carmel) and were guided
by Carmelite sisters. This had not, however, proved possible in Jerusalem
and the nuns at Mt Carmel had arranged through the Franciscans of St
Saviour's for them to be guided through the Holy City by a friar. Thus the
portion of their pilgrimage in which I participated was somewhat less
orientated towards the specificities of their group work and its institutional
contexts than was the rest of their pilgrimage, when they were guided by
leaders more closely affiliated with their association.

The friar's presentation of the holy places, and the interaction of the
pilgrims with those places, was very different from analogous presentations and relations on Greek Orthodox pilgrimages. Like Orthodox

guides, the Franciscan presented secular and historical information about places outside the chapels built to commemorate them (but not, as with the Orthodox guides, off the property of the holy places). However, when inside, he continued to instruct the pilgrims and talked not of the site itself but of the significance of what was alleged to have occurred there. Thus, inside the mosque which encloses the traditional site of Christ's ascension, Father Raphael read two biblical passages pertaining to the ascension (Matthew 28: 16 and Luke 24: 50) before telling the people that 'what is important is not the literal place but the actual fact of the ascension'. The pilgrims and the friar then engaged in a discussion of the significance of the ascension during which one woman said that the footprint of Jesus, enshrined within the mosque, 'is not relevant, it is only there to assist us in the interiorization of the significance'. The group then recited the Lord's Prayer and a series of ten 'decades' ('Hail Marys') after which Raphael read the *virs Galilee* passage from the Gospels and added that 'we should stop staring at the sky and get on with the missionary call of Christ'.

This pattern of drawing spiritual inspiration from a site and directing its significance back into activity in the world continued through other sites in and around the Old City. Each place had a particular significance, not only linked to what was alleged to have happened at that site but also to the way that event provided inspiration and a model for devout activity in the pilgrims' lives. When available, as they usually were in Latin holy places, realistic wall paintings of the events which the places commemorated were pedagogically mobilized. Details of the representations were pointed out and expanded upon so that the pilgrims could interiorize the event, which was usually drawn from the gospels. (At St Saviour's friary, the headquarters of the Franciscan Order in the Holy Land, the lives of St Francis and his followers were set up as models of inspiration.) The event was then given contemporary moral significance, and the pilgrims were pointedly told to go into the world and get on with applying the lesson to their lives in it.

Whereas the Orthodox approach to the holy places diminishes the specificity of the places by grouping them as manifestations of Paradise, the Catholics diminish the specificity of the sites by distinguishing between the significance of the biblical events said to have happened at the sites and the places themselves. It is from the significance, not the places, that one draws inspiration, and the places serve primarily as *loci* where the pilgrims are better able to body forth the subjects of their meditations in their imaginations. Thus, in Franciscan sites in particular, there are full-scale, dramatically painted presentations of the holy places' events: the Chapel of the Flagellation on the Via Dolorosa is particularly striking as its life-size paintings of Christ's judicial humiliation are designed, with the help of painted plaster extensions, to project out of the walls and into the space of the chapel itself. Pilgrims can, in effect, place themselves in the presence of these events while in the chapel and can thus be particularly moved by their experience.

None the less, the experience of interiorization can take place away from the sites; it is the image, not the place, which is important. I noticed, on the many occasions I accompanied Catholic pilgrims on Friday processions along the Via Dolorosa, that they invariably kept their eyes closed in prayer as the friars who led the processions read out the appropriate Gospel passages; several pilgrims told me that they did not want images of the literal place to get in the way of the images of Christ's procession that they normally meditated on when they performed the Stations of the Cross in their home churches. During the Little Way pilgrimage, crowds along the Via Dolorosa prevented our party from stopping at many of the traditional sites of the Stations of the Cross. We would pass by them, with Father Raphael simply pointing out the markers. Later, when a doorway or a courtyard was available, we would step inside and the monk would carefully take us through Bible readings pertaining to the sites we had passed (and those we were about to pass), present meditations on those sites, and lead the people in their decades and their prayers. The friar's words, and memories of their devotions at the Stations of the Cross within their home churches, provided the pilgrims with the foundations on which to build their reflections.

An unplanned alteration in the Little Way's itinerary revealed the primary role of the church, through its officiants and its rituals, in mediating between God and its members. It is, finally, the liturgy, in which officiants sanctified by God through the agency of the church pass on to celebrants the redemptive power of the blood and flesh of Christ, which puts believers into communion with God. Meditations and devotions serve to make clear to them the debt owed to Christ and the consequent necessity of orientating their thoughts and actions towards his will, but it is only through the channels of the liturgy that the spiritual orientation can be translated into a real and redemptive contact with God.

We were supposed to have a communion mass at the Franciscan chapel of Dominus Flevit (which commemorates the site at which Christ wept for the imminent destruction of Jerusalem), but we arrived at the chapel an hour before our scheduled time. Father Raphael managed, after considerable effort, to get permission for us to have mass instead in a small chapel (redolent with the fumes of cabbage being cooked for the friars' lunch) attached to a nearby building in which the attendant friars lived. I had noted that, up to this time, the pilgrims had shown curiosity at the sites we had visited but not, surprisingly, displays of strong emotion, even at places commemorating events quite signal in the career of Christ. However, during mass this coolness dissolved. The pilgrims spent the half-hour on their knees, with three of the women crying throughout and several of the others breaking into tears during communion. It was there, in a chapel with only an incidental connection to the holy places and during a mass identical to those they engaged in at home, that the pilgrims seemed most to feel the presence of Christ and, in that presence, tearfully and indiscriminately embraced all the members of their group.

PROTESTANT PILGRIMAGE

Protestant devotions in the Holy Land, for reasons both historical and ontological, tend to be disengaged from the traditional holy sites revered by the Orthodox and the Catholics. Protestants came late to the Holy Land, and the claims of the more well-established churches to significant places, made official by the Ottoman firman, or edict, of 1852, were firm and well monumentalized. Furthermore, the Protestant desire to have an unmediated relation to the Bible means that a holy place covered over with Orthodox or Catholic churches is, in effect, a site which commemorates institutional domination rather than the truth which that institution has usurped and distorted. Protestants, in general, approach the Holy Land for the same inspirational reasons as Catholics, but for them that inspiration devolves from what is interpreted as an unimpeded relationship between the individual and Christ and not, as with Catholicism, from the sense of being part of a long history during which the will of Jesus has been enacted in the world through the agency of the church. Consequently, Protestants tend to want to witness Christ himself and not his putative agents, and prefer to frequent places, such as the area around the Sea of Galilee or the Garden Tomb in Jerusalem where they can imagine Christ in situ, rather than monuments thrown up by two thousand years of devotion to his memory.

The Garden Tomb saliently displays the characteristics of Protestant Holy Land devotion. The tomb, which many Protestants consider the actual site of Christ's burial, is a small enclosed site outside the walls of the Old City within which there is a careful reconstruction of a rich man's garden of the first century AD. Louring over this quiet orchard of olive and carob trees is a rock face which is given the appearance of a skull by the open sockets of two eroded medieval cisterns. The Garden Tomb guides, trained volunteers who are the only persons allowed to guide people while they are within the garden's confines, instruct visitors that the site before them is identical to that described in the biblical texts which present Christ's crucifixion and entombment. They point out that the site is correctly located outside the walls (although they fail to mention that the contemporary walls of the Old City, built in 1542 by Suleiman the Magnificent, are very differently placed from those of the city within which Jesus was condemned and outside which he was crucified). The skull-like hill above it is obviously Golgotha, 'the place of the skull', and the garden itself appears to be the garden of the wealthy land-holder, Joseph of Arimathea. Whether or not they are convinced that the Garden Tomb is the literal site (and there is occasional dissension on this issue), pilgrims assert that 'it is easier to imagine Jesus here than inside that dark pile of stones they call the Holy Sepulchre'.

During one of my visits to the Garden Tomb, I accompanied a group of evangelical Christians from the Assembly of God Church of Lakewood, California, through the garden, into the tomb itself and then to a small garden area where they had communion and a 'praise meeting'. During the meeting, the wife of the minister announced to the people that, while she was in the tomb, she herself saw 'the grave clothes thrown back and the angel at the door who said "Why do you seek the living among the dead?" [Luke 24:5]. "He is not here, for He has risen." [Matthew 28:6]'. She then proceeded to tell the congregation that since she, and they, have 'today seen that the tomb is empty, we know that everything the Bible says is true. We must live according to its word.'

Within Protestantism the concept of 'living according to the biblical word' has a wide range of reference, calling upon some sects to separate themselves as far as possible from the secular world so as to organize personal and communal lives around biblical precepts, while demanding of others that their members labour in the fields of political activism to impose their readings of biblical morals on the whole of the world around them. One influential strain of biblical fundamentalism, developed under the influence of the Scofield Bible, has promoted a reading of scriptures which relates all biblical prophecy to historical events which will occur in the final days preceding Christ's Second Coming. Within this movement, believers argue that their divinely ordained task in the world is to work to bring about that Second Coming and, with it, the destruction of the fallen world and all those who, because they have not worked to effect the return of Christ, do not merit salvation.

Christian Zionists, who make up a small but influential sector of this tendency, have organized themselves around readings of several Old and New Testament books (principal among them Jeremiah, Ezekiel, and Ephesians) which, they believe, call on them to bring God's chosen people (the Jews) back from the distractions of diaspora to rebuild the kingdom of Israel within its biblically mandated borders ('from the Nile to the Euphrates') and re-establish the Solomonic Temple and its ordained rituals. Christian Zionists believe that this work, which – 'because we are now living in the "final" days' – is to be done now, will bring Christ back into the world where he will engage in battle and destroy the Anti-Christ (who will rise in the Soviet Union) and thus bring about the millennium and the rule of God in the world. Merv Watson, a spokesman for the International Christian Embassy (a non-denominational pressure group established to effect the work of Christian Zionism), told me in an interview that 'our role is to speed up the day in which the ultimate destiny of the day is realized....If our faith is anything it's not just nodding our heads to prophecy but getting off our butts to do something to help'.

The annual Feast of Tabernacles pilgrimage to Jerusalem is organized by the Embassy to bring fundamentalist Christians to 'Eretz Israel' where they can 'comfort' the Jews and witness the work of God. It is, like other Latin pilgrimages, inspirational in that it serves to reveal to participants that the Embassy's work is divinely ordained and is, despite the demonic opposition of other churches, secular humanists, communists, and Arabs, succeeding in transforming the world. Here inspiration does not, however, entail visiting the sites of Christ's historical life and death but in seeing the way that Christ, through his workers in the contemporary world, is preparing the way for his return.

There was very little travel involved in the week-long celebration in which I participated in 1984. On free afternoons people could join guided trips to Israeli settlements on the occupied West Bank where they would see the 'Jews laying claim to the land God gave them' or could go to religious schools where fundamentalist Jews were being taught how to perform the rituals of sacrifice in preparation for the time when the Temple is re-established on the current site of the Al-Aqsa mosque and the Dome of the Rock. Most of the week, however, was taken up by meetings within the West Jerusalem Binyenei Ha'ooma convention hall where lectures on God's work in Israel and the world by Jewish and Christian 'tools of God's fulfilment' were punctuated with prayer meetings and healing sessions.

The lectures ranged widely within parameters set by the necessity of understanding and witnessing God's intervention in contemporary history. We were addressed by biblical scholars who told us how to understand the Bible in the light of current world and Israeli politics, by 'Fishers of Jews' who described their work of preaching to Jews in the Soviet Union the urgent need for them to emigrate to Israel and dedicate themselves to building up the state, by representatives of the Jerusalem Temple Foundation who spoke of the necessity of levelling the Muslim holy places on the Temple Mount so that the Judaic Temple could be re-established, and by officials of the Embassy who instructed us on how to mobilize support for Israel's 'redemptive mission' when we returned home.

The fact that this meeting sounds more like a political workshop than a pilgrimage belies neither its religious character nor its affinity to Orthodox and Catholic pilgrimages. All the pilgrimages examined here function through enabling pilgrims to feel they are integrally, and to a degree exclusively, involved in the divine redemptive project. For the Orthodox, that project is most evident in the presence of images which 'transfer the event from the terrestrial world in which it had occurred to the celestial' (Talbot-Rice and Talbot-Rice 1974: 93) and in so doing temporarily carry the observer there as well. In Catholicism, the engagement of pilgrims in the worldly work of the church, an engagement effected by their participation in its rituals and institutional frameworks, links them more closely with God. For Christian Zionists God's work is manifest in the fate of the kingdom of Israel and projects, like the Feast of Tabernacles, which enable them to feel that they, and the others who surround them, are integrally involved in bringing about what God wills for Israel and the world.

The Christian Zionist celebration of the Feast of Tabernacles is a means by which fundamentalist Protestants locate themselves within the history of the Jewish people and unite themselves with a project which is, by their lights, the core of God's redemptive work in the world. Their seven days of dwelling in West Jerusalem hotels and gathering together in a foreign convention centre coincide perfectly with the seven days of the Jewish *Succoth* (celebrated simultaneously throughout Israel) during which Jews, as the Bible instructs, 'shall dwell in booths... that your generations may know that I made the people of Israel dwell in booths when I brought them out of the land of Egypt' (Leviticus 23: 42–3). During those seven days in 1984 the Christian Zionists presented and analysed strategies for bringing to an end the present-day exile of Jews and 'spiritual Jews' (the term by which one of the speakers, George Giakamakos, citing Romans

9–11, referred to the assembly) and 'conquering' the messianic kingdom promised to them by God.

The culmination of the week's celebration of the Feast of Tabernacles was a 'Praise Procession' meant to enact before the eyes of the Israeli people the 'coming up of the nations to Jerusalem' (Leviticus 23: 33–6, 39–43) and to celebrate with them the finish of the Judaic *Succoth*. The marchers, grouped by nation of origin, waved banners and palms and sang the praises of Israel and the imminence of Christ's return as they processed noisily along the route to be followed by the Messiah when he returns to take up his kingdom (from the top of the Mount of Olives to the foot of the Western, or Wailing, Wall). At the finish of the march Jan Van der Hoeven, one of the Embassy's officials, instructed the pilgrims to 'go down to the Western Wall and pray' and, while the majority engaged in this ritual of identification, one small group of Americans, led by a tele-evangelist, convinced an elderly Hassidic Jew to read to them, in Hebrew, from the Torah. When he finished the reading the old man laid his hands on the leader's head and, in Hebrew, blessed him. Then the leader returned the gesture, saying in English, 'The Lord bless you'. At this the whole group, eyes clenched in what appeared to be ecstasy, waved their hands in the air and began to chant 'Hallelujah, praise the Lord'.

CONCLUSION

Jerusalem pilgrimage forces the anthropologist to look at its practices as complex interweavings of discourses on the nature of God, history, and humankind at sites designed to give those discourses concrete form in the world. The multiplicity of its practices, which devolves from the diversity of interpretative communities which construct those discourses, makes Jerusalem pilgrimage appear anomalous with respect to the single de-nomination pilgrimages which to date have informed the theoretical apparatus of the anthropology of pilgrimage. I contend, however, that Jerusalem pilgrimage is not aberrant but instead most saliently illustrates the discursive construction of all pilgrimages. Pilgrimages are journeys to the sacred, but the sacred is not something which stands beyond the domain of the cultural; it is imagined, defined, and articulated within cultural practice.

To comprehend pilgrimages in the particularities of their practices, anthropologists must explore the many disparate sites at which concepts of the sacred, and desires to engage it, are forged. Such exploration may carry anthropologists far from the scenes where pilgrimages are enacted, for it is at the sites whence pilgrims set out on their searches for the centre that pilgrims learn what they desire to find. At the centres where they go in expectation of fulfilling that desire pilgrims experience little other than that which they already expect to encounter.

REFERENCES

Anderson, P. (1974) *Passages from Antiquity to Feudalism*, London: New Left Books.
Asad, T. (1983) 'Anthropological conceptions of religion: reflections on Geertz', *Man* 18: 237–59.
Barthes, R. (1975) *S/Z*, trans. R. Miller, London: Cape.
Berlière, U. (1890) 'Les pèlerinages judiciaires au moyen age', *Revue Bénédictine* 7: 520–6.
Brown, P. (1964) 'St Augustine's attitude towards religious coercion', *Journal of Roman Studies* 54: 107–16.
Brown, P. and MacCormack, S. (1982) 'Artifices of eternity', in P. Brown (ed.) *Society and the Holy in Late Antiquity*, London: Faber & Faber, pp. 207–21.
Campbell, J. (1964) *Honour, Family and Patronage: A Study of Institutions and Moral Values in a Greek Mountain Community*, Oxford: Clarendon Press.
Clifford, J. (1988) *The Predicament of Culture: Twentieth Century Ethnography, Literature, and Art*, Cambridge: Harvard University Press.
Constable, G. (1976) 'Opposition to pilgrimage in the Middle Ages', *Studia Gratiana* 19 (1): 123–46.
Dix, G. (1945) *The Shape of the Liturgy*, Westminster: Dacre Press.
Dumont, L. (1982) 'A modified view of our origins: the Christian beginnings of modern individualism', *Religion* 12 (1): 1–27.
Frend, W. H. C. (1971) *The Donatist Church: A Movement of Protest in Roman North Africa*, Oxford: Clarendon Press.
_____ (1984) *The Rise of Christianity*, London: Darton, Longman & Todd.
Gibbon, E. (1914) *History of the Decline and Fall of the Roman Empire*, ed. J. B. Bury, London: Oxford University Press.
Herrin, J. (1987) *The Formation of Christianity*, Oxford: Basil Blackwell.
Hirschon, R. (1989) *Heirs of the Greek Catastrophe: The Social Life of Asia Minor Refugees in Piraeus*, Oxford: Clarendon Press.
Kamenka, E. (1973) 'Political nationalism: the evolution of the idea', in E. Kamenka (ed.) *Nationalism: The Nature and Evolution of an Idea*, Canberra: Australian National University Press.
Lea, H. C. (1896) *A History of Auricular Confession and Indulgences in the Latin Church*, Philadelphia: Lea Brothers.
Talbot-Rice, D. and Talbot-Rice, T. (1974) *Icons and their Dating*, London: Thames & Hudson.
Ullmann, W. (1970) *The Growth of Papal Government in the Middle Ages*, London: Methuen.
Vogel, C. (1964) 'Le pèlerinage pénitentiel', *Revue des Sciences Religieuses* 38 (2): 113–53.
Watkins, O. D. (1920) *A History of Penance*, London: Longman.

Chapter five

Place and person in Sinhala Catholic pilgrimage

Richard L. Stirrat

INTRODUCTION

Over the last few decades, there has been a shift in emphasis in Catholic pilgrimage in Sinhala Sri Lanka. After the consolidation of the Catholic church in Sri Lanka in the nineteenth century, the great centres of pilgrimage consisted of a series of places defined by the clergy and the laity as sacred places (*sidhasthanaya*), where the power of the divine could be tapped by humanity. During the last couple of decades, however, new shrines have developed. Here, place is sometimes still important, but of much greater significance have been the particular people around whom the shrines revolve. These 'holy men' are seen as being imbued with the power of the divine, and it is their presence at these shrines which makes them centres for pilgrimage. In this chapter, I shall be examining this change of emphasis and suggesting some of the factors which might help us understand this shift from place to person as the focus of pilgrimage in Sinhala Catholicism.

Catholicism was introduced into Sri Lanka by the Portuguese in the sixteenth century. As long as the Portuguese were the dominant power along the Sri Lankan littoral, Catholicism was the privileged religion in areas under their control. When the Portuguese were replaced by the Dutch, Catholics became subject to Protestant persecution, which ended only with the advent of British rule at the end of the eighteenth century. During the British period, missionary priests from France and elsewhere consolidated the Catholic community, creating a strong sense of identity, partly through the encouragement of pilgrimage (Boudens 1979). Through an excellent system of schools and an informal network of contacts, Catholics became a relatively privileged minority in the country. After independence in 1948, the position of this Catholic minority rapidly declined in the face of Sinhala Buddhist resurgence (Caspersz 1974;

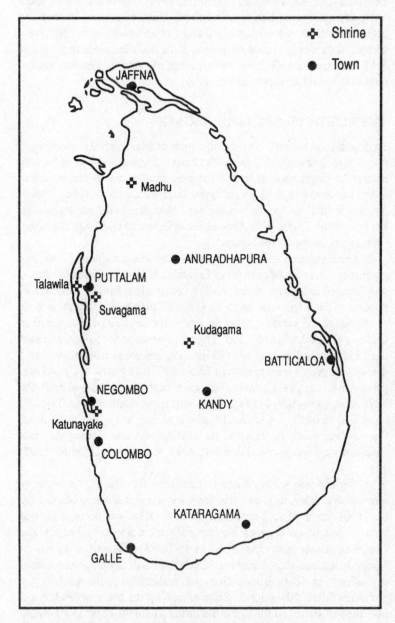

Figure 5.1   Principal Catholic shrines of Sri Lanka

Dharmadasa 1988; de Silva 1977; Stirrat 1984). The schools were taken over; attempts were made to discriminate against Catholics in access to higher education and jobs, while foreign missionaries were effectively barred. Today, only around 6 per cent of the Sinhala-speaking people of Sri Lanka are Catholic, most of them concentrated in a narrow coastal strip to the north and south of Colombo.

THE RISE OF PILGRIMAGE SHRINES

During the nineteenth century, the missionaries actively encouraged pilgrimage. Throughout Catholic Sri Lanka, particular churches became centres for pilgrimage. Most of these were small-scale affairs, attracting a few hundred people from the immediate area, and providing opportunities for the missionaries to address larger than usual congregations; but two shrines, those of St Anne at Talawila and of Our Lady at Madhu, became pre-eminent (see Figure 5.1).[1]

St Anne's church at Talawila stands on the western shore of Kalpitiya peninsula, about 85 miles north of Colombo. It is claimed that the shrine was founded in the seventeenth century, but the first hard evidence for its popularity dates from the later years of the Dutch period. By the middle to late nineteenth century, Talawila was by far the most popular shrine in Catholic Sri Lanka. In 1857, 8000 pilgrims were reported to have attended the main feast in July, and by 1895 the local government agent estimated that 40,000 people were present (Modder 1908). To put these figures into perspective, the total Catholic population in the island according to the 1895 census was under 215,000. Well into the twentieth century, Talawila continued to be the pre-eminent Catholic shrine in the country. Indeed, the numbers attending Talawila far outstripped those visiting the main Buddhist pilgrimage centres of Sri Lanka at that time (Modder 1908: 171).

A slightly less ancient history is claimed for Madhu. In the early nineteenth century, it appears that there was a minor shrine at Madhu. By the 1830s, it was of sufficient importance for it to have become a major bone of contention between the European missionaries and schismatic Oratorian priests from Goa (Boudens 1979: 88). Thereafter, the rise of Madhu to national importance was largely the result of European missionary efforts. In 1870, Bishop Bonjean, presumably influenced by the growth of Marian devotion in Europe, took up the cause of Madhu and instituted an annual pilgrimage to the shrine (Boudens 1979: 159; Fernando 1938: 13). By the 1930s, Madhu had overtaken Talawila in popularity, and through the thirties and forties it was claimed that up to 250,000 pilgrims were attending the various feasts in honour of Our Lady.

For the pilgrims who flocked to these shrines, their great attraction was the miraculous power they were claimed to possess. The earliest detailed descriptions of Talawila, by W. C. Mcready, the Assistant Government Agent for the area in 1867, described people buried up to their necks in the open sand in front of the church in the hope of miraculous cures. Others were tied to crosses, 'their arms outstretched well above their heads. They were also afflicted in some way or other and looked to St Anne for relief' (*Ceylon Government Administration Reports* 1867: 66–8). A few years later, Bishop Joulain described how 'the speciality of the St Anne pilgrimage is the number of possessed who come to be freed. It would appear that St Anne has a very special power over the devil.'

From Madhu, too, there are detailed descriptions of miraculous cures. The earliest of any note dates from 1905 and describes the exorcism of a woman possessed by a demon (Lewis 1917: 180). As at Talawila, the possessed were tied to crosses and buried in the ground in the hope of miraculous cures. Such miracles formed the basis for the popularity of these shrines. They were visible proof that these were supernaturally charged sites where the divine was truly manifest in the material world, and thus the faithful travelled to the shrines for other reasons: to gain the help of saints, to fulfil vows, or simply to gain grace.

The missionaries themselves were somewhat ambivalent about these 'miracles'. Some aspects of what they saw at Madhu and Talawila were to them little more than idle superstition, yet they too believed in the miraculous qualities of the shrines (Lewis 1917: 180). Furthermore, they saw the shrine pilgrimages as opportunities through which a life of faith could be deepened and interiorized, and for this reason Bishop Bonjean's successors, Bishops Melizan and Joulain, continued to encourage pilgrimage to the sites. At the same time, both Madhu and Talawila were important sources of income for the church, and not surprisingly the emerging dioceses of nineteenth-century Sri Lanka squabbled over their jurisdiction (Boudens 1979: 56).

Yet if miracles of exorcism and curing gave visible proof of the sacred power inherent in these shrines, what was seen as the basis of this power? In what events and in what physical forms was this power inherent? Here, it seems, what was important was place.

Looking first at the myths of origin of the two shrines, both stress the particular nature of the sites. Taking Talawila first, there are two myths which tell of the shrine's beginnings. The first, and the most common, refers to an impoverished Portuguese traveller who fell asleep under a tree at Talawila. He had a vision of St Anne, who presented him with a relic in the form of a statue, gave him money, and instructed him to build a shrine in her honour at the spot of his vision. Another story tells of a shipwrecked sailor, once again Portuguese, who hid his statue of St Anne in a tree at Talawila. He made a vow to return if his business prospered, and fulfilled his vow by building the original church there (Anandappa n.d.: 245-6; Pieris 1950; Stirrat 1982: 391-2).

The stories surrounding the foundation of Madhu are slightly different (Stirrat 1982: 393-4). A favourite one tells of a man travelling through the jungle who heard a call from a tree. Looking up, he saw a statue of the Virgin and heard a voice instructing him to build a chapel for the statue. Another story tells of how the statue was found in the *bund* of an old irrigation tank at Madhu, while the most popular ones link the origins of the shrine to the Dutch persecution of Catholics. In the eighteenth century, so it is told, a statue of the Virgin was taken from the coast inland in order to escape the attentions of the Dutch. It was kept at Madhu, and miracles began to take place. Slowly, people realized that the statue had miraculous powers, and when attempts were made to take it back to its original home, it refused to move. On this basis, so it is claimed, Madhu began to rise to fame.

It is notable how similar some of these stories are to those reported from Catholic Europe concerning the origins of pilgrimage shrines. This is a point to which I shall return later. What I want to emphasize here is how all these stories stress in one way or another the importance of place. Thus, the stories concerning Talawila stress the conjunction of the particular place with the traveller's rest or the sailor's shipwreck. Those concerning Madhu tell of how the statue was found at the shrine, or how, once it had been brought there, it refused to move. In all these stories, the actual identities of the persons who had the visions are unimportant: their names are unknown.

This stress on place also crops up in other contexts. Thus, at both shrines, those seeking miraculous cures were buried in the soil of the shrine. Furthermore, even today what is important at both Madhu and Talawila is the soil. In Madhu church, there is a grave-like hole in the floor from which pilgrims scoop sand to take home, the sand being replenished daily during the feasts (Collin 1917: 193; Lewis 1916: 124). At Talawila, the sand is simply taken from the area around the church.

More generally, as I have shown elsewhere (Stirrat 1982), the symbolic structure of these shrines and of pilgrimage to them depends upon the manipulation of space. Put very briefly, the siting of these shrines in what to the Sinhalese is the 'jungle' places them in opposition to the 'village', opposing the wild to the domestic. Yet at the same time, the organization of space at these shrines represents a moral hierarchy, the untamed jungle being the domain of amoral and evil forces, and the centres of the shrines – the churches – being the domain of the omnipotent and the all-good sacred. The intermediate zones afford space for the re-creation rather than the negation of normal social life.

Thus, space and place are integral qualities of these two traditional pilgrimage shrines in Catholic Sri Lanka. Space and place are used to create a hierophany through which humanity can meet the divine and tap its power. Pilgrimage in this context is concerned with the movement to a particular place which is considered divinely chosen and imbued with the sacred. Indeed, the place is a manifestation of the divine.

Over the last two decades or so, however, Madhu and Talawila have declined in importance. As I indicated earlier, Madhu had overtaken Talawila in popularity by the 1930s, but the absolute number of pilgrims appears to have continued to grow at both shrines until the 1950s. Even today both shrines, particularly Madhu, attract enormous crowds,[2] but there has been a change in attitude towards them. Increasingly, people deny that they have the divine powers with which they were thought to be imbued. Many of those who go to these shrines describe their visits as being concerned primarily with pleasure rather than with religious fervour. Those for whom religious motives are still strong describe their visits in terms of which the nineteenth-century missionaries would have approved: deepening their spiritual lives, rather than searching for miraculous powers and benefits. For the many who still seek divine help and miracles, new shrines have developed, and these are focused not on places but on persons.

PERSON-CENTRED SHRINES

The most famous of these new shrines is that of Our Lady of Lourdes in a small village called Kudagama. This is centred on a priest called Father Jayamanne, who is considered to have a very special relationship with the Virgin Mary. As I have discussed this shrine at some length elsewhere, however (Stirrat 1977, 1979), I here briefly describe some other new Catholic shrines.

Suvagama is the name given to a small shrine outside the town of Puttalam, about 80 miles north of Colombo. Here, a young man known as Brother Lambert officiates over the rituals of healing and devotion. He, rather than Suvagama, is said to be favoured by the divine, in this case the Virgin Mary.

Like many of the holy people of contemporary Catholic Sri Lanka, Lambert describes his childhood as one of hardships and privations. Born in poverty, he claims to have early developed a particular devotion to the Virgin Mary, and as a child he wanted to become a priest. His family, however, was too poor to send him to the seminary, so Lambert held a number of low-paid and boring jobs. After a series of particularly gruelling episodes, he began to have visions and dreams of the Virgin. She announced that she had chosen him for a special task: to heal the sick and, through the miracles he would perform, to lead people back to the true religion. She also equipped him with a miraculous rosary, but told him that it would be miraculous only when in his hands.

In the early 1980s, Lambert began his ministry. He claims that, at first, he was derided by both the laity and the priesthood, but when he healed people his fame began to spread, and even the local clergy had to admit, albeit grudgingly, the efficacy of his powers. He started to erect a number of buildings on a piece of scrubland owned by his family, and began to develop a complex of rituals held each weekend at his shrine. By the time I met Lambert, he was attracting hundreds of devotees each weekend, who attended various novenas, the Way of the Cross, and the blessings which he gave the pilgrims.

It would be wrong to say that place has no importance at Suvagama. The ritual area of the shrine is marked off, and within its confines such activities as smoking and drinking are rigorously barred. This is the only Catholic shrine I have come across in Sri Lanka where devotees have to remove their shoes before entering. As at Madhu, devotees take soil from the shrine as a prophylactic against demonic attack. Yet the sacred qualities of the shrine do not exist independently of Brother Lambert. Rather, they depend upon his presence, and without him the shrine would cease to exist. Because he is favoured by the Virgin Mary, therefore, the place within which he resides is imbued with his qualities. Thus, if he leaves the shrine, he carries these powers with him. A visit from Brother Lambert is equivalent to a pilgrimage to Suvagama.

This stress on person is perhaps more clearly seen at other new shrines. At one, that of Our Lady of Katunayake, the focal character is a man who styles himself Bishop Aponsu. Like Lambert, Aponsu had wanted to be a priest but failed to complete his time in the seminary. He too experienced a series of visions, culminating in his ordination by Christ himself. Each weekend, hundreds of devotees attend the shrine and take part in its rituals. Bishop Aponsu is widely regarded as having divine powers, particularly those of healing the physically and demonically afflicted. Amongst those who come to the shrine, there is no importance whatsoever attaching to place; all that is important is Bishop Aponsu, his stigmata, and the powers he has been granted by Christ. At another shrine, an individual named Norbert is possessed on a weekly basis by St Sebastian, and while possessed can carry out supernatural cures (Stirrat 1981). Once again, there is no stress laid on the physical location of the shrine: all that is important is the person of Norbert.

In sum, then, while place cannot be totally discounted in these new shrines, there is a change in emphasis. In all of them, the focus of attention is a particular person who in himself embodies in one way or another the power of the divine. This power travels with him rather than being tied to a particular spot, as in the older shrines. *People* rather than *places* embody the sacred, and pilgrimage is a matter not of visiting a particular site but rather of seeking out a particular individual. Moreover, these individuals are themselves mobile. The foci of pilgrimage can, and sometimes do, visit the pilgrims.

THE SHIFT FROM PLACE TO PERSON

In understanding this shift in the nature of the pilgrims' goal, a number of separate aspects are identifiable. Some are closely associated with developments internal to the Catholic church and with changes in the situation of the church in contemporary Sri Lanka. Other factors appear to owe less to the specificities of Catholic Sri Lanka and more to processes affecting all religious groupings in the country. All, however, reinforce one another to give rise to the shift from older shrines focused on place to newer shrines focused on persons.

One of the features of both Talawila and Madhu alluded to earlier is their close association with the clerical hierarchy in the country. Dioceses once fought over their jurisdiction, and since at least the last quarter of the nineteenth century have exercised increasing control over the behaviour of pilgrims (Lewis 1917).[3]

The church was keen to harness the efficacy of these shrines in order to enhance its own legitimation. Furthermore, by stressing the importance of place, such centres were relatively easy to control, much easier than the occasional individual who claimed a direct, personal relationship with the divine. Indeed, the European quality of the myths of origin of both

Madhu and Talawila may well have been part of a deliberate strategy to facilitate such a stress on place, as well as reflecting an attempt to bring the pilgrimage centres of Sinhala Catholics into a Eurocentric tradition of Catholicism (Turner and Turner 1978). Finally, the miracles which took place at Madhu and Talawila were visible proof of the power of the church, proof that the hierarchy really did have God on its side, and that Catholicism was the true religion.

However, in the last twenty to thirty years a number of factors have undermined both the position of the hierarchy and the status of these shrines. Internal to the church have been the reforms of Vatican II, which have led to a shift in the hierarchy's view of what is 'true' Catholicism. The type of religiosity encouraged in the past is now attacked as idle superstition, or at least as a backward form of Catholicism. Pilgrimage to Madhu and Talawila has been discouraged and presented as less important than other forms of devotional activity. Behaviour at the shrines has been more rigorously controlled and claims to miraculous events denied.

Second, the position of the Catholic community in Sri Lanka has changed. From being a privileged minority who saw their success as a just reward for their faith, Catholics now feel themselves to be an oppressed and occasionally persecuted group. For many, the hierarchy is to blame for this decline. On the one hand, they failed to stand up to Sinhala Buddhist pressure; on the other, they failed to remain true to traditional Catholicism and thus to ensure the continued support of the divine.

The result of these two processes has been that the legitimacy of the church, particularly as seen in the character of the present hierarchy, is now open to question by the laity. While obedience to the teachings of the church led to material advantages for Catholics and the miracles of curing at Madhu and Talawila, today there are no miracles and modern Catholicism brings no worldly benefits. Because Madhu and Talawila are so closely associated with the hierarchy, their legitimacy is also open to question. Many Catholics now see them as nothing more than tourist centres; while once they were sacred places, today people go for little more than recreation, and lurid stories circulate about what goes on in the jungle around Madhu. The decline in the legitimate authority of the church and its present-day lack of effective means of control means that new shrines can develop, in a sense filling the void left by the decline of the old.

Thus, at Katunayake and Suvagama, frequent criticisms are made of the church and specifically of shrines such as Madhu and Talawila. In a rather self-conscious fashion, the claim is made at all these new shrines that the divine has intervened to persuade the laity to return to traditional Catholicism. The institutional church is derided as having abandoned its principles – at times of even being a tool of the devil. Only at these new shrines, so it is claimed, is true Catholicism practised, and only through them can the faithful receive the favours of the divine.

Yet such an argument which limits itself to processes affecting only the Catholic church and the Catholic population of Sri Lanka is limited. Of course, there is a sense in which the declining legitimacy of the church and the decreasing authority of the clergy have allowed forms of religious expression to develop which previously would have been nipped in the bud. What is striking, however, is that the developments in Sinhala Catholicism have their analogues in developments among other religious groupings in Sri Lanka, most notably among Sinhala Buddhists. Indeed, it is in the Buddhist context that one can most easily perceive the processes I wish to highlight.

RELIGION AND POLITY IN SRI LANKA

The 'traditional' system of pilgrimage in Sinhala Buddhism involved various distinct elements.[4]

One of these elements was pilgrimage to the great shrines of Sinhala Buddhist civilization, but another, of more relevance in the present context, involved a hierarchically conceived set of shrines associated with the gods. In Sinhala Buddhism there has always been an intimate relationship between religion and the polity. This is clearly seen in a number of ways, most significantly in the congruence in modern Sri Lanka between the pantheon of the deities and the organization of the state. The Kandyan kingdom in some ways resembled what Weber called a 'patrimonial state'. Authority and honour in theory flowed from the centre down through a hierarchy of officials, and their position depended upon this downward flow. Similarly, the pantheon of gods was organized as a parallel hierarchy through which authority flowed and which encompassed gradations of morality. Central to both was the concept of *varam*, delegated authority. With the growth of electoral politics, the metaphor began to change: the world of the gods began to be talked of, at least by some, not in terms of the king and the patrimonial hierarchy but in terms of the prime minister and his ministers. Again, there was a congruence between the secular polity and the world of the gods.

One of the most pronounced features of the Sri Lankan polity since independence has been the development of various systems of patronage.

On leaving Sri Lanka, the British attempted to create a political system based on the Westminster model, in which one of the crucial features is a strong distinction between policy making, the job of the members of parliament, and policy implementation, the task of a politically neutral administration. Whether it ever worked effectively is open to question, but certainly the gap between ideal and practice soon widened.

The development of a patronage system in post-colonial Sri Lanka depended upon a number of factors. First, in reaction to the heavily westernized bureaucracy, post-independence governments attempted to make the administration more responsive to the desires of the electorate by giving members of parliament more and more power. Increasingly, MPs began to control access to and distribution of the resources of the state. Second, the dismal performance of the Sri Lankan economy and its failure to cope with the rapidly growing population and the rising aspirations of the rural masses meant that MPs could use this control over resources to reward past loyalty and to attract future support.

The result of these various processes has been that MPs have become powerful patrons surrounded by sets of personalized, dyadic ties which exist autonomously from all other relationships. Indeed, a feature of all patron–client systems is the presence of such isolated, unmediated, dyadic relationships. This is what places such systems apart from bureaucratic or patrimonial systems of delegation, in which each relationship is represented as part of a wider system of relations. Second, the value which is emphasized in these patronal relationships is loyalty. Followers should be loyal to their patron; the patron should be loyal to his followers. The ideal is reciprocity, with each party considering the exchange balanced, and this of course causes problems for the MP. Third, the system operates as a zero-sum game, or at least this is how it is seen. If X receives patronage, it is at the expense of Y. If X is loyal to A, he cannot be loyal to B. Finally, it is a system which stresses persons rather than rules or statuses. What one gets, whether one wins or loses, depends upon personal ties.

Returning to religion, this change in the nature of the polity appears to be what underlies one of the most dramatic developments in Sinhala Buddhism: the rise of the shrine of Kataragama (Handelman 1985; Obeyesekere 1977, 1978, 1981; Pfaffenberger 1979; Nissan 1988). In the past, the god Kataragama was simply one of a number of guardian deities, but since independence his stature has grown to such an extent that he now overshadows all the other gods, and literally hundreds of thousands of pilgrims visit his shrine each year. The great attraction of Kataragama is that he exemplifies all the qualities of the ideal patron. He has no interest in moral issues: in return for loyalty, he will produce the goods. Today, rather than existing within a hierarchical pantheon, he stands alone. Furthermore, Kataragama has become the focus for devotional forms of religiosity in which exclusivity and a personal relationship with the deity are stressed above all else. Kataragama has become the patron *par excellence*.

In the case of Sinhala Catholics, the situation is rather different. In the first place, there was never the same congruence between the polity and the pantheon of saints. In a sense, the ecclesiastical hierarchy of the church played the same function for Catholics that the hierarchy of gods played for Sinhala Buddhists. Moreover, none of the saints has quite the same amoral qualities displayed by Kataragama, although St Anthony of Padua runs him quite close at times. However, there are parallels. First, there has been a tendency for exclusive devotions to grow and for saints to lose their particular, specialized functions. Thus, many Catholics have developed particular devotions to particular saints, turn to these saints for help in all matters, and view their relationship with them in highly personal terms. Second, there has been a dramatic rise in the frequency of sorcery accusations among Sinhala Catholics.[5] In the past, misfortune was commonly interpreted as the result of attack by capricious demons, but such demonic attack is now seen as being due to sorcerers working for clients. Here, then, the causes of success and failure are seen as the result of personalized forces, rather than as the outcome of luck, of abstract powers, or of the imposition of administrative rules. Dealing with sorcery is one of the most important reasons that bring people to the new Catholic shrines.

Perhaps the most obvious result of this stress on the personalistic, however, is the rise of the holy men around whom these new shrines revolve. Men like Brother Lambert and Bishop Aponsu embody in themselves divine power which is in no way dependent upon the church. They personalize the divine just as MPs personalize the state. They have been chosen because of who they are as individuals, and not because of their position in some more encompassing structure. Within such a frame of reference, place loses its importance. For what the concentration on place allows is control by the ecclesiastical hierarchy, and in the present-day Sri Lankan context an emphasis on place would symbolically reassert the role of the church as mediator. From the beginning of the Catholic presence in Sri Lanka, the church has been closely involved in politics. In today's political climate, however, both in terms of the position of Catholics in the country and in terms of the way the polity works, a stress on place ceases to have much relevance. Instead, what is important is the person, and the holy men of the Sinhala Catholics embody what the MPs desire: the infusion of the divine which makes them unique.

Given this process, it is not surprising that the people who flock to these new shrines in the greatest numbers are those from social strata which rely most heavily on patronage links. Few of the pilgrims at Suvagama or Kudagama come from fishing or agricultural areas, where the power of the MP is relatively limited. Rather, they are of middle-class backgrounds or from urban areas, people for whom getting a job or obtaining housing depends on whom one knows. The majority come not out of any great spiritual need but for mundane, down-to-earth reasons: getting employment, dealing with court cases, recovering stolen property, and dealing with the effects of sorcery. Whereas in the past the priest could provide such services, nowadays he is increasingly powerless, his role usurped by the holy man.

CONCLUSION

What I have tried to show in this chapter are some of the forces which have led to a decline in the popularity of shrines where place is stressed, and the rise of shrines focused on the person. I have suggested that one crucial factor in this change has been the way in which the Sri Lankan polity has been transformed since independence. Of course, what I have been describing is, in part, an age-old theme in Catholic history: the tension between the church and ecclesiastical attempts to control mediation between humanity and the divine on the one hand, and individuals who claim a direct contact with the sacred on the other. Here, I have been concerned with how this tension is manifested in one small corner of the Catholic world, and how the fragmentation of the Sinhala polity has been accompanied by the fragmentation of the Catholic church itself.

NOTES

The fieldwork on which this chapter is based was supported by the Economic and Social Research Council, the Leverhulme Trust, and the British Academy, to all of whom I express my gratitude. A somewhat different version was presented to the Department of Anthropology, University of Virginia, and I thank those present for their comments. Finally, as ever, I must thank E. Nissan and J. Perkins.

1 A much fuller discussion of these shrines appears in Stirrat 1984.
2 The numbers at Madhu, however, have fallen in recent years with the increase in conflict between the Sri Lankan government and Tamil separatists for, given the location of Madhu, people are afraid to go there. Furthermore, the splits between Tamil and Sinhala Catholics have also reduced the number of Sinhala Catholics visiting the shrine (see Stirrat 1984).
3 At Talawila, there were even priests known as 'disciplinarians' whose role it was to maintain seemly behaviour and good order.
4 There is a vast literature on Sinhala Buddhist pilgrimage; see, for instance, Gombrich 1971; Nissan 1985, 1988; Obeyesekere 1963, 1966; Swearer 1982.
5 For a similar development among Sinhala Buddhists, see Obeyesekere 1975.

REFERENCES

Anandappa, J. B. C. (n.d.) *The Catholic Directory of Sri Lanka 1975–76*, Colombo: Catholic Bishops' Conference of Sri Lanka.
Boudens, R. (1979) *Catholic Missionaries in a British Colony*, Immensee: Nouvelle Revue de Science Missionaire.
Caspersz, P. (1974) 'The role of Sri Lankan Christians in a Buddhist majority system', *The Ceylon Journal of Historical and Social Studies* NS 4: 104–10.
Ceylon Government Administration Reports (1867), Colombo: Government Printers.
Collin, J. (1917) '"Madu" or "Madhu"', *Ceylon Antiquary and Literary Register* 2: 193.
de Silva, K. M. (1977) 'The religions of the minorities', in K. M. de Silva (ed.) *Sri Lanka: A Survey*, London: C. Hurst.
Dharmadasa, K. N. O. (1988) 'Buddhist resurgence and Christian privilege in Sri Lanka, c. 1940–1965', in K. M. de Silva, P. Duke, E. S. Goldberg, and N. Katz (eds) *Ethnic Conflict in Buddhist Societies*, London: Pinter.
Fernando, S. J. (1938) *The History of Madhu Church*, Colombo: privately published.
Gombrich, R. (1971) *Precept and Practice*, Oxford: Clarendon Press.
Handelman, D. (1985) 'On the desuetude of Kataragama', *Man* 20: 156–8.
Lewis, J. P. (1916) '"Madhu" again', *Ceylon Antiquary and Literary Register* 1: 124.
_____ (1917) 'Some folklore from the Northern Province', *Ceylon Antiquary and Literary Register* 2: 179–81.
Modder, F. (1908) *Gazetteer of the Puttalam District of the North-Western Province of Ceylon*, Colombo: Frank Cottle.
Nissan, E. (1985) 'The sacred city of Anuradhapura: aspects of Sinhalese Buddhism and nationhood', unpublished Ph.D. thesis, London School of Economics, University of London.
_____ (1988) 'Polity and pilgrimage centres in Sri Lanka', *Man* 23: 253–74.
Obeyesekere, G. (1963) 'The great tradition and the little in the perspective of Sinhalese Buddhism', *Journal of Asian Studies* 21: 139–53.
_____ (1966) 'The Buddhist pantheon in Ceylon and its extensions', in M.

Nash (ed.) *Anthropological Studies in Theravada Buddhism* (South East Asia Studies 13), New Haven: Yale University Press.

———— (1975) 'Sorcery, premeditated murder and the canalization of aggression in Sri Lanka', *Ethnology* 14: 1–23.

———— (1977) 'Social change and the deities: the rise of the Kataragama cult in modern Sri Lanka', *Man* 12: 377–96.

———— (1978) 'The fire-walkers of Kataragama: the rise of *bhakti* religiosity in Buddhist Sri Lanka', *Journal of Asian Studies* 37: 457–76.

———— (1981) *Medusa's Hair*, Chicago: Chicago University Press.

Pfaffenberger, B. (1979) 'The Kataragama pilgrimage: Hindu–Buddhist interaction in Sri Lanka's polyethnic system', *Journal of Asian Studies* 38: 253–70.

Pieris, E. (1950) *Talawila Santana Maniyo hevat Talawila Sidhasthanaya Puravruttiya*, Chilaw: Saint Peter's Press.

Stirrat, R. L. (1977) 'Demonic possession in Roman Catholic Sri Lanka', *Journal of Anthropological Research* 33: 122–48.

———— (1979) 'A Catholic shrine in its social context', *Sri Lankan Journal of the Social Sciences* 2: 77–108.

———— (1981) 'The shrine of St Sebastian at Mirisgama', *Man* 16: 183–200.

———— (1982) 'Shrines, pilgrimages and miraculous powers in Roman Catholic Sri Lanka', in J. W. Sheils (ed.) *The Church and Healing*, Oxford: Oxford University Press.

———— (1984) 'Catholics and the riots in historical perspective', in J. Manor (ed.) *Sri Lanka in Change and Crisis*, London: Croom Helm.

Swearer, D. (1982) 'The Kataragama and Kandy Asala Peraharas: juxtaposing religious elements in Sri Lanka', in G. R. Welbon and G. E. Yocum (eds) *Religious Festivals in South India and Sri Lanka*, New Delhi: Manohar.

Turner, V. W. and Turner, E. (1978) *Image and Pilgrimage in Christian Culture: Anthropological Perspectives*, Oxford: Basil Blackwell.

Chapter six

Pilgrimage and cultural fracture in the Andes

Michael J. Sallnow

INTRODUCTION

When people converge in pilgrimage, meanings collide. The mere fact of a mass gathering at a sacred site is unlikely to indicate any unanimity of meaning or motive among the participants; on the contrary, it is more likely to reveal severely discrepant or discordant understandings of the significance of the cult, even among those nominally sharing the same faith. Such understandings, fashioned and elaborated in specific historical and cultural milieux, might be articulated into contradictory and perhaps competing discourses concerning the shrine and its origins, significance, and powers, with such discourses validating different sets of devotional practices. Invariably, a particular discourse will receive for the time being the stamp of approval and orthodoxy from the cult officialdom, while others might be marginalized, disdained, or even suppressed; but over time, elements of the authorized discourse and its associated practices might in their turn come to be repudiated by the cult staff, passing into the non-official, popular stratum of cultic meanings and activities. This hierarchization and transformation of cult discourses cannot, of course, be understood apart from the wider social and historical contexts out of which the cult has emerged, and within which it persists.

This chapter pursues these reflections in relation to pilgrimage in the South American Andes. In one perspective, Andean pilgrimage, being nominally Christian and Roman Catholic, is but an historical offshoot and local development of the European pilgrimage tradition. In another perspective, however, it appears as a quite distinct phenomenon, comprehensible only in terms of the pre-Hispanic, colonial, and post-colonial histories of the region. Pilgrimage, more so perhaps than any other form of religious practice, discloses the peculiar, internally contradictory character of Andean Christianity, and indeed – as I shall argue – of Andean culture as a whole.

The data on which this chapter is based derive chiefly from ethnographic fieldwork among Quechua peasants in the Cusco region of southern Peru, and from archival research in Cusco. The analysis would probably hold good throughout the central Andean area, but there is a dearth of published material with which to substantiate this. The data utilized here have for the most part been published elsewhere (Sallnow 1974, 1981, 1982, 1987, 1990), and I therefore restrict myself to outlines and summaries of the main points.

HISTORICAL BACKGROUND

Andean culture has a pilgrimage tradition stretching back a millennium before the birth of Christ. Between 1000 and 500 BC the oracular cult of Chavín gained preponderance over a wide area of the sierra and Pacific littoral, stimulating inter-regional traffic and exchange on a scale unknown thitherto. Its powerful priesthood was evidently able to mobilize vast armies of labourers, but the cult does not appear to have been associated with a state organization as such. Its influence gradually fell away, and it was not until the second half of the first millennium after Christ that new inter-regional shrines arose, this time linked directly or indirectly to the formation of the first Andean states. Chief amongst these shrines were Tiwanaku, on the altiplano south of Lake Titicaca, which became the centre of a far-flung theocracy in its own right as well as lending religious impetus to the militaristic Wari state further north; and Pachakamaq, on the coast south of modern Lima, which, though never possessing an independent political base, became the focus of a pilgrimage network ramifying throughout the central Andes as far as the tropical forest to the east, and which indeed outlived those shrines whose cults were married to more immediate political and military concerns.

With the rise of the Inka empire in the fifteenth century, existing local, regional, and provincial shrines were co-opted by the Cusco conquerors into a centralized religious geography focused on the imperial capital, with shrine effigies lodged in a pantheon in the temple of the Sun. Pilgrimage, as the bodily mapping of socio-religious space, reached its apogee in those Inka imperial rituals which united all the shrines of the dominion through the medium of human sacrificial blood, transported in its living victims or in sacred vessels between Cusco and the provincial centres along radial lines or *ceques*, the metaphorical arteries of the state.

The Spanish conquest of the central Andes brought in its wake a three-stage religious colonization. First, Marian and other saintly images were installed as the divine patrons of this or that ethnic group, in the belief that loyalties to the corresponding pagan tutelars would wither on the bough. This optimism was belied by the millenarian crisis of Taki Onqoy in the 1560s, in which the neglected indigenous deities, formerly lodged in features of the natural landscape such as mountains, crags, and rivers, came to occupy the bodies of cult adepts, speaking through them and predicting the imminent overthrow of the white invaders and their gods.

Following the suppression of the Taki Onqoy, Spanish religious colonization entered its second phase. Vigorous campaigns for the extirpation of idolatry were belatedly launched. At the same time, the wider native ethnicities were obliterated and the population resettled in *reducciones*, nucleated villages, and *doctrinas*, Indian parishes, each with its own local, exclusive repertoire of saints, fiestas, and *cargos*, circulating ritual offices.

This second phase, that of cult localization, brought in its train a third phase – that of cult regionalization. From the closing decades of the sixteenth century onwards, certain Christian statues or images began to be hailed as miraculous, being credited with bringing rain, opening springs, healing, granting miscellaneous favours, or with having mysteriously appeared in some locale. It was these miraculous shrines, many of them controlled by religious orders, that became the foci of pilgrimage. They typically hallowed indigenous sacred sites, or at least were located in the latter's precincts. It is no coincidence that two of the earliest and most popular colonial pilgrimage shrines, both Marian advocations, were established in the environs of Tiwanaku and Pachakamaq respectively.

THE SHRINES

At first sight, it might seem that Andean pilgrimage shrines were – and are – European, and more specifically Hispanic, transplants judiciously lifted by a proselytizing clergy to a fertile South American soil. They are all recognizable advocations of standard figures of the Christian pantheon, and have annual pilgrimages and fiestas on their appropriate days in the Roman liturgical calendar. Their diagnostic characteristic is their innate miraculousness, a quality which refers either to the circumstances of their original appearance, or to their continuing prodigious powers, or to both. Many of these shrines, though by no means all, are situated away from the main residential centres, sometimes in isolated places difficult of access. The majority are staffed on a permanent or *ad hoc* basis by

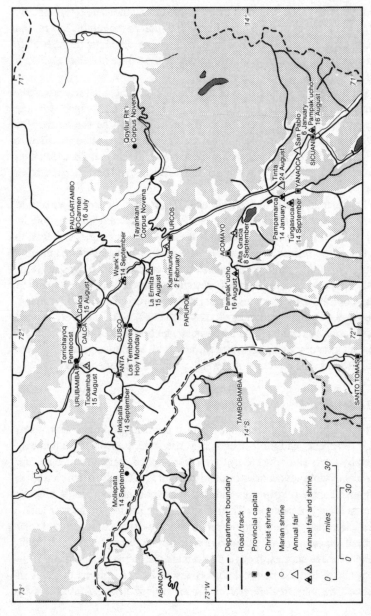

Figure 6.1 Principal shrines of the Cusco region, southern Peru

Catholic priests; some have become the nuclei of monastic communities, and the cults of these shrines generally follow an orthodox liturgy. In all these respects, Andean pilgrimage shrines bear comparison with their Iberian counterparts, the more ancient and important centres dating from colonial times being analogous to inter-regional Spanish sanctuaries such as Guadalupe and Montserrat, and the lesser and more recently founded ones being comparable with the regional and inter-local shrines described by Christian for the Nansa valley of northern Spain (Christian 1972).

These Spanish examples, however, highlight an interesting initial divergence between Andean and European pilgrimage centres. Whereas in Spain, as in the rest of Catholic Europe, pilgrimage shrines are over-whelmingly Marian, in the Andes, as elsewhere in Latin America, the Virgin shares the stage with Christ himself, represented chiefly, though not exclusively, in the advocation of the crucifixion. Now the enshrining of Christ became popular in Spain during the seventeenth and eighteenth centuries (Christian 1981), and was accordingly exported to the New World at the same time. But while most of the European Christ-shrines are now defunct as pilgrimage centres, their Andean counterparts continue to flourish. In the Cusco region, indeed, Christ-shrines outnumber Marian ones (see Figure 6.1). The interesting question here, I would submit, is not so much why shrine-centred devotion to Christ has persisted in the New World, but rather why in Europe it has been so decisively ousted by Mariolatry.

Where the Andean shrines begin to depart at a more fundamental level from the European pattern is in their connections with an indigenous cosmology. Many shrines, as already mentioned, were established at or near indigenous sacred sites. There is nothing particularly unusual or surprising about this: the early Christianization of Europe proceeded in a similar fashion, as a result of a deliberate strategy on the part of mission-aries who anticipated a simple transfer of religious sentiments from pagan idol to Christian icon. Whereas in Europe this is largely a matter of historical interest, however, in the Andes it is of direct and continuing relevance for understanding contemporary religious practice.

The Andean landscape is imbued with sacredness. Human destinies are in part determined by chthonian powers, localized in the spirits of mountains, rocks, springs, rivers, and other topographic features, and generalized in the earth matrix, Pachamama. The cult of these telluric deities meshes with the cult of the dead, and has as its principal goal the channelling of the variegated powers inscribed in the landscape, pre-eminently the power of fertility, towards the satisfaction of human interests. This indigenous substrate to contemporary Andean religion is emphatically not a cultural survival from the pre-Columbian past, as is so often alleged; on the contrary, it has been actively reproduced and transformed, along with the peasant mode of livelihood which it serves, by the structures of political domination and economic exploitation imposed by the colonial and, later, the republican state.

The Christian advocation of a pilgrimage shrine, because of its direct insertion into – perhaps one should say its emergence from – this animate landscape, is irredeemably compromised. Through its determinate localization, through its unique anchorage to a particular spot on the Andean terrain, its acknowledged thaumaturgic powers begin to merge and fuse with the powers of the chthonian deities. In this respect, miraculous shrines are quite different from the local patron saints of communities and villages, celebrated annually on their days with masses, processions, and fiestas. These local divine tutelars, allocated to the various villages by the colonial ecclesiastical authorities, are for the most part expressly non-miraculous: their cosmological role is unstressed, and their cults are observed as a matter of routine. They serve as local emblems of inclusion and exclusion, of division and union, of hierarchy and subordination, but – for peasant devotees at least – they are largely devoid of symbolic content, whether orthodox or syncretist.

Miraculous shrines, on the other hand, are replete with symbolic meanings, expressed through such media as myth-histories of origin, miracle stories, iconology and so forth, all of which tend either implicitly or explicitly to combine Christian and indigenous notions of divinity. In this way, the standard saints and personages of the Catholic pantheon are subtly or overtly 'Andeanized', transformed into uniquely identifiable sacred figures distinct from their namesakes in the Old World.

This fusion of meanings lends to the Andean case a complexity which cannot easily be comprehended within the dual model of official versus popular religion habitually applied to European Catholicism (e.g. Vrijhof 1979). Orthodoxy, after all, is situational. While, in a European context, shrine-centred devotion might be classed as 'popular' in contrast to a more cerebral, generalized devotion, in the Andes it is likely to be thoroughly esteemed by its practitioners as a sublimated, official form of Catholic worship in contradistinction to the 'folk' practices of the less enlightened. This distinction is invariably couched in the pervasive ethnic idiom of 'mestizo', literally 'mixed race' but nowadays connoting an orientation towards Hispanic cultural mores, versus 'indígena', Indian. Furthermore, such devotional fault lines frequently inhere in the same cult. A miracu-

-lous shrine, by its very nature, is a repository of conflicting, contradictory meanings vested in it and exploited by different sections of its cultic constituency – priest and layman, governor and governed, town dweller and country dweller, landlord and peasant. Such conflicting meanings might co-exist in uneasy coalition, or different sets of meanings might gain the ascendant at different times. A miraculous shrine is, in a very real sense, an arena of competition and struggle between different groups attempting to win control of a crucial cultural resource.

Some specific examples will illustrate this point. The urban shrine of El Señor de Los Temblores, Lord of the Earthquakes, in Cusco city, for instance, which became a focus of cult following the devastating earthquake of 1650, is in one aspect that of a Christ for the urban poor. Its carved wooden face, darkened by candle-smoke, is said to have an authentic Andean complexion, unlike the standard Caucasian colouring of most religious images. In 1834, the cathedral authorities provoked widespread discontent by retouching the Temblores crucifix, for it was believed that a white *taytacha* (Quechua 'little father', the term applied to all images of Christ) would no longer work miracles. Yet despite its obvious demotic appeal, the shrine is squarely in the civic domain. The lay brotherhood which controls the cult and its considerable finances recruits from the ranks of the urban élite, while its Holy Week fiesta is an occasion for a joint parade of the entire episcopal hierarchy, military commanders, and city aldermen.[1]

The rural shrine of El Señor de Qoyllur Rit'i, Lord of the Snow Star, situated in an isolated coomb beneath a ring of glaciers some 70 kilometres east of Cusco city, encapsulates tensions which are even more acute. The shrine was allegedly established on the basis of divine apparitions to a young shepherd-boy at the spot, in the wake of a widespread but unsuccessful rebellion against the colonial authorities in the 1780s. It is an image of the crucified Christ painted on a rock, petrification being a characteristically Andean form of theophany. It is explicitly associated by peasant devotees with the spirit of nearby Mount Ausankati, the most powerful mountain deity in the region. Accordingly, it has the reputation of being a thoroughly 'Indian' shrine, imbued with a telluric power which makes it a particularly successful miracle worker. Yet the shrine's current wave of popularity was initiated by the blessing of the retouched image by the archbishop of Cusco in 1944, and it has subsequently been controlled by a lay brotherhood whose members are drawn from the rural élite and who see themselves as '*mestizo*' in contrast to the broad mass of 'Indian' devotees. The members of the brotherhood maintain an officious presence throughout the titular fiesta of the shrine during the Corpus novena, carrying rope whips which they do not hesitate to use on devotees whom they consider to have shown disrespect for the shrine or who have committed some ritual infraction. Devotees might also themselves ask to be ceremonially whipped as a penance. The archbishop of Cusco now regularly presides over the fiesta, in a shrewd attempt to co-opt the cult to the ecclesiastical mainstream. Furthermore, while it is still a favourite pilgrimage destination for thousands of highland peasants, over the last few years there has been a marked increase in the number of urban, middle-class pilgrims. Culted by both prelate and peasant, Qoyllur Rit'i combines – albeit uneasily – impeccable Catholic credentials with the immanent power of the animate landscape.

A third example is that of El Señor de Wank'a, Lord of the Crag, situated not far from Cusco city on the slopes of the Vilcanota valley, the main transport artery of the region. The shrine is again a lithic image, this time of Christ being scourged, an advocation known as Cristo de la Columna. Alleged to have originated from the vision of an Indian fugitive in the late seventeenth century, the figure is said to have appeared to a wealthy mine-owner some decades later, and to have cured him of an intractable disease. Its healing powers began to be promoted by its Mercedarian custodians during a virulent epidemic in the early eighteenth century, and it has remained popular ever since. A large regional fair is now held to coincide with its titular fiesta on the feast of the Exaltation of the Cross in September.

In the last fifty years or so, the Mercedarian priests have striven to purge the Wank'a cult of what they see as Indian practices such as ceremonial music and dancing, and have courted a more sophisticated, urban clientele by building roads to the shrine and constructing more salubrious sleeping quarters for the pilgrims. They even downplay the healing power of the shrine, omitting any reference to it in their sermons and stressing instead the message which the iconography holds for the Christian life – respect for authority and the dignity of suffering. They utilize, in other words, a predominantly sacrificial discourse in contrast to the miracle discourse espoused by the majority of worshippers.

Not surprisingly, given the iconography of the shrine, flagellation has a central place in the Wank'a cult as well. Here, however, it is self-administered by the devotees themselves, at prescribed times in the evenings of the fiesta octave and novena when the lights in the shrine complex are switched off. The priests disdain such ostentatious devotional exercises, but are obliged by popular demand to allow them to continue, albeit under cover of darkness.

As a result of the priests' proscriptions, there are now few community peasants among the 20,000 devotees at the Wank'a fiesta. However, at least two other, minor Christ-shrines in the vicinity schedule their fiestas on exactly the same day, to attract Wank'a's disenfranchised peasant constituency. One of these peripheral shrines has for its advocation Christ as the just judge, Justo Juez, thereby neatly transforming the theological-cum-political meanings of the Wank'a Christ as a model for obedience and suffering into the much more radical symbolism of Christ as dispenser of justice on behalf of the oppressed (cf. Sallnow 1982). In this case, the inherent contradictions in the original cult have led to its schism into a number of different cults, iconologically and liturgically linked but catering for different clienteles.

This last example leads to a related point of contrast between miraculous shrines in the Andes and their European counterparts. It has to do not so much with the intrinsic characteristics of the shrines themselves as with the relationships which are premised between them. Peasant informants tend to perceive miraculous shrines not individually but as members of sets, generally of three, four, or, most often, five Marian or Christological shrines.[2] The membership of these sets varies from place to place through a given region. The usual pattern is for a set to include both nearby, minor shrines and more distant, major ones, and to predicate relations of sibling-ship between them.

Typically, it is said that five brother *taytachas* were wandering through the area, and that each stopped to rest at the spot where his shrine now stands, the oldest first and the youngest last. The members of a set are therefore ranked in order of fraternal seniority, corresponding to a hierarchy of miraculous power. Such a locally focused shrine set does not necessarily include all miraculous shrines of which members of a particular community or locality are cognizant, although those which it does include tend to be more highly regarded as pilgrimage venues; the set also changes its composition over time, as new shrines rise to prominence and others sink into disuse. Church officials dismiss these beliefs as, at best, naive folklore and, at worst, woeful misunderstandings of the mystery of the Trinity.

These contemporary, ethnocentric shrine sets had their pre-Columbian counterparts in the sub-imperial patterns of pentads of kindred *wak'as* (sacred sites) described in the sixteenth-century Quechua narrative from Huarochirí, in the central Peruvian highlands (Avila 1598). The wandering *taytachas*, meanwhile, are directly reminiscent of the itinerant sons of Viracocha, the creator god/culture hero of sixteenth-century Andean mythology. The shrine sets are, in effect, the cognitive complement to the act of pilgrimage: they serve as mental devices for modelling geo-ritual space, for generating shifting ethno-regions about fixed local centres in a manner partly independent of the centripetal systems of political and religious control. It is noteworthy, for instance, how few of these shrine sets include El Señor de Los Temblores in Cusco city, the administrative and ecclesiastical centre of the region throughout the Inka, colonial, and republican epochs. The apparently haphazard meanderings of the brother-Christs stake out a ritual territory within which human pilgrims from a particular community – who are also, as we shall see, deemed to be brothers and sisters to one another – make their own, determinate peregrinations.

THE CULTS

Turning to the organization of Andean pilgrimage, we have to contend with a variety of styles and motives. At the annual festivity of any important regional pilgrimage centre, one encounters devotees who have made the journey alone or with a few friends or relatives, and who are attending purely for personal reasons, seeking material favours or simply spiritual grace from the shrine divinity. One might also encounter parish or village groups, neighbours, and acquaintances who have travelled together and who might have a tradition of annual visits to the sanctuary. At certain shrines – El Señor de Wank'a, for example – these pilgrim groups are formally organized as local branches of an *hermandad*, brotherhood; at the shrine they parade beneath their embroidered banners, and senior officials of the brotherhood police the processions and religious services. Members of the sodality are guaranteed masses at the sanctuary when they die, provided their subscriptions are up-to-date. These forms of pilgrimage organization resemble the standard European forms, and are generally manifested by those devotees, both urban and rural, enjoying or laying claim to *mestizo* status and professing what they see as orthodox Catholicism.

There is, however, another, distinctively Andean mode of pilgrimage, stereotypically associated with peasant pilgrims from the upland communities. It entails an annual community *cargo*, or office, for each shrine visited, that of *patrón*, sponsor, technically allocated like all religious *cargos* to a married man but in practice discharged by the husband and wife jointly. The sponsoring couple is responsible for recruiting or hiring ceremonial dancers and musicians for the occasion; they must also feed for the duration of the pilgrimage the dancers, musicians, and all the other pilgrims who choose to join the party, and are obliged to feast them lavishly on the eve of departure and following their return. By successfully discharging these obligations, the sponsors earn honour and prestige in the eyes of their fellow community members.

The ostensible purpose of a pilgrimage organized in this way is to escort a small portable icon, known as a *lámina* or *demanda*, from the community to the shrine and back. The contingent is called a *nación*, meaning 'tribe' or 'nation': the party from the community of Qamawara, for example, would refer to itself as the '*nación de Qamawara*'. This was the term used by the Spaniards to denote the various native ethnic groups in the Andes in the years immediately following the conquest. After the crisis of the 1560s, as already noted, native ethnicities were suppressed in favour of a single category of *indígena*, 'indigene'. The retention of the term '*nación*' in the context of pilgrimage is thus highly significant. It suggests that when the peasant-pilgrims leave their home territory and head across the mountain trails for a miraculous shrine, they cease for the time being merely to be representatives of a depressed and dependent hinterland community, but are temporarily transformed into a unique Indian nation. Their ethnic identity is redoubled: they are Indian both in the sense of a unified and subordinate category of the colonial and neo-colonial state, and also in the sense of being native to a specific locale, anchored by birth and ancestry to a particular tract of the animate landscape.

For this reason, participation in *cargo*-type pilgrimage carries an ethnic loading far greater than does the celebration of local fiestas, pervaded as they are by metaphors of ethnic hierarchy and subordination. To participate in such a pilgrimage is to acquiesce in a deeper consciousness of Indianness, one no longer relative but absolute, a consciousness of an identity springing – it would seem – not from historically contingent relations of politico-economic power but instead from an inalienable birthright to a socio-geographic niche in an enduring sacred landscape.

The passage of the *nación* across the landscape to the shrine is heavily ritualized. Ideally, the journey should be made on foot, although for longer pilgrimages a truck is invariably taken for part of the way. Members must march in compact single file and must sit in a tight circle when resting, in case evil spirits should intrude. The route is marked by prayer-stops at the first coigns of vantage of sacred mountains and miraculous shrines, and is interrupted by random encounters with other *naciones* with whom it is obligatory to engage in reciprocal veneration of *láminas*. On the outward journey all these procedures and rituals are observed assiduously, but on the homeward trek, with the party disorganized and many of the pilgrims drunk, they are frequently ignored.

The ethos of the *nación* is aggressively egalitarian. All members are said to be brothers and sisters to one another, and loads, chores, food, drink, and lodging are allocated equally without discrimination. Yet, paradoxically, this egalitarianism is sustained only by the absolute authority of the leader, the head of the ceremonial dance troupe. All members of the party, the sponsor included, are obliged to defer to him. Moreover, mutualism stops at the boundaries of the *nación*. Between *naciones* there is neutrality tinged with competitiveness, evidenced by the jealous territoriality of *naciones* camped in the shrine precincts, by informal virtuoso contests between their bands of musicians, and occasionally by brawling and outright physical violence.

Central to a *cargo*-type pilgrimage are the ceremonial dancers. I cannot here describe and analyse the many dance styles currently favoured by Andean devotees; suffice it to say that each style has its own costume, symbolism, choreography, music, and instrumentation, and that many have come to acquire associations of either rusticity or sophistication, construed once again in terms of the Indian–*mestizo* opposition. Each sponsor selects a principal dance style for his *nación*, being guided partly by tradition and partly by personal taste. A dance troupe goes through its routines at the critical points of the pilgrimage – the entry and exit of the *lámina* at the sponsor's house, at the shrine sanctuary, and at any lodgings *en route*. The musicians, however, typically play their instruments almost continuously throughout the pilgrimage, so that the entire journey has a surreal, dance-like quality.

In a double sense, ceremonial dancing is a synecdoche for the entire pilgrimage. The dancers are proxies for all members of the *nación*, and their formal, choreographed sequences are synoptic of the journey as a whole. For Andean peasants, a visit to a miraculous shrine is undertaken not just in order to pursue some private request to the shrine divinity, nor merely to satisfy social obligations and to earn the esteem of one's fellows. Both these ends may feature as motives, but the means to achieve them is an end in itself. Pilgrimage, above all, is a kinaesthetic mapping of space, a charting by bodily movement of the contours of the religious landscape as they rise upwards from the peripheral homelands of the *nación* to a sacred centre, a specially hallowed site where Christian divinities have begun to fuse with the telluric Andean powers. The journey itself is the crucial component of the enterprise: the ritual passage of the peasant-pilgrims across the terrain is a symbolic re-appropriation of the all-powerful, animate landscape by its rightful denizens.

PILGRIMAGE AS NEO-COLONIAL RECLAMATION

The theological disjunctions and devotional discordances in contemporary Andean pilgrimage cults have their immediate origins in the diametrically opposed colonial discourses provoked by the emergence of the first miraculous shrines in the region. When Christ and the Virgin Mary began to manifest themselves in the Andes through apparitions and miracles, their devotees vested the prodigious occurrences with radically different interpretations. For the Spaniards, they provided incontrovertible proof that their conquest had been divinely vindicated, and that the Christian God was finally wresting the New World from the hands of Satan. It was the ultimate, conclusive phase of colonization, the impregnation of a foreign and diabolic landscape by the known and trusted divinities from home. The miraculous apparitions and manifestations, at once wondrous and comfortingly familiar, reconsecrated and domesticated the alien territory in the name of Christ and delivered it to his Spanish crusaders.

For the native Andeans, however, the phenomena conveyed an altogether different meaning. To them, they signified that the innate sacred powers of the landscape were now working not just through the familiar spirits of mountains, crags, and springs, but through the medium of these imported *wak' as* as well. Moreover, since many of the native regional shrines had been destroyed in the campaigns for the extirpation of idolatry, the sites of these new theophanies – frequently the old pagan sites iconologically refurbished – quickly acquired immense popularity amongst the Indian population. The colonial period, indeed, was the golden age of Andean pilgrimage (Kubler 1946: 361).

From the outset, then, miraculous images enshrined a fundamental, theological contradiction. For the Spaniards, they were the vehicles for displacing the satanic perversions of native religiosity and for reclaiming a foreign land for their faith and their God. For the Indians, on the other hand, they were the means to domesticate the foreign gods, to insert these evidently powerful divine interlopers into the matrix of the animate landscape and through them to reclaim and to re-appropriate the extra-local sacred and ritual dimension of their colonized territories. Each group perceived and misunderstood the behaviour of the other through the inverting lens of its own understandings. Thus, the Spanish clergy could and did construe devotional pilgrimage on the part of Indians as evidence of their conversion to Christianity. The Indians, for their part, construed pilgrimage by Spaniards as demonstrating a tacit recognition by the colonists of the power of the animate landscape. Out of this mutual misinterpretation of motives, in which both conquerors and conquered each saw their own religious sensibilities reflected in the behaviour of the other, there arose a chronic indeterminacy as to what these miraculous shrines did actually signify. Over time, with the blurring of racial and cultural boundaries brought about by migration and intermarriage, such shrines came to mean largely what the varied constituencies of their multifarious devotional catchments wanted them to mean – albeit within, though sometimes outside, the more or less rigid constraints of the discourse propagated by the prevailing cult officialdom.

Colonial pilgrimage, then, reveals itself as the epitome of the cultural fracture established by the Spanish conquest, a fracture that has been perpetuated down to the present day by the entrenched political and economic structures of domination and exploitation. It is a fracture which runs through every aspect of contemporary Peruvian highland society. The racial idiom of *mestizo* versus Indian casts all the complexities of cultural practice into a grossly simplified, ethno-historical framework in which a Hispanic tradition is seen to be in perpetual confrontation with an indigenous one. The contrast is relativistic, its contents continually shifting and changing with a fine disregard for historical fact; but its form is constant. This persisting ideology of conquest, still in place nearly five centuries after the event, is congruent with, and serves to legitimate, a political order that has consistently maintained two classes of citizenry – until very recently, for example, literacy (in Spanish) was a requirement for voting – and with an economic order which has reproduced a subsistence peasantry in order to subsidize, with undersold labour and produce, the capitalist system which encapsulates and impoverishes it.

Contemporary Andean pilgrimage appears in this perspective, then, as a double act of reclamation: claiming the territory for God and the universal church, and reclaiming it for its place-specific sacred powers. These two opposed yet inseparable theological orientations inhere in every miraculous shrine of Christ and the Virgin Mary and are, respectively, loosely aligned with the two broad devotional styles of individual and *cargo*-type pilgrimage. The act of pilgrimage, however, in common with all social practice, is multiform: it inevitably catches up the alternative, sub-dominant meanings in each case, as well as the central, dominant ones. The result is a complex, dialectical interplay of meanings and practices in which everything appears as double-edged and self-contradictory. Thus, private pilgrimage by sophisticated urban devotees is not only a Catholic quest for the grace or favour of Christ or the Virgin, but also a demonstration of an implicit commitment to a belief in the power of the animate landscape. Conversely, the peasant members of a *nación* are not only tracing with their bodies the geo-religious connections between their home territories and the key sources of chthonian power, but are also implicitly subscribing to the Christian idiom of devotional penance and saintly intercession. Each devotional package, so to speak, necessarily entails its culturally constructed antithesis: the dual connotations are inescapable.

These two sets of theological meanings and ritual practices, however, are not so much diacritic of discrete and mutually exclusive groups as the indices of nothing less than a split cultural identity. Pilgrimage casts into especially sharp relief the enduring puzzle for contemporary Andeans of who they really are. Thus, the devotional code is susceptible to apparent dissimulation and to complicated inflection. Urban pilgrims are most likely to travel as private individuals or in parish groups, while community peasants invariably attend as *naciones*. However, *mestizos* from provincial towns and villages might visit the more important shrines as formally constituted *naciones*, though with dance troupes of carefully selected *mestizo* styles, thereby validating their claim to a qualified but authentic local cultural identity. An Indian peasant, on the other hand, might choose to make an individual penitential pilgrimage, going through the correct pietistic routines at the shrine and thereby demonstrating an orthodox, *mestizo* religious sensibility.

Given these inversions and uncertainties, it is hardly surprising that among the more heterogeneous pilgrimage congregations of the major miraculous shrines, there is much finessing of social boundaries, achieved by means of selective interaction, insult and innuendo, and strategic displays of cultural competence, especially in language – either Spanish or Quechua, depending upon the image being projected. Not immediately evident is the psychological discomfiture engendered by a practice laden with such acute cultural contradictions, though this does occasionally break the surface, for example in drunken protestations of 'real' identity, either 'Indian' or 'Peruvian'.

I have endeavoured in this chapter to show that Andean pilgrimage, despite its similarity to European pilgrimage in certain respects, can be properly understood only by placing it within the successive pre-Columbian, colonial, and neo-colonial contexts from which it has emerged. I have argued that it presents itself today as an epitome of the chronic cultural schizophrenia that afflicts Peruvian highland society. To claim and reclaim a colonized sacred landscape for human purposes is to claim and reclaim a compromised cultural identity. Miraculous shrines in the Andes, with their hierarchical organization, their dual theological orientations, and their contrasting devotional styles, preside over the imposition, manipulation, and defence of vitally significant, ethnic-cum-ethnohistorical frontiers – frontiers which not only differentiate class from class, group from group, and person from person, but which are also directly inscribed within individual psyches.

NOTES

The fieldwork on which this chapter is based was funded by a Foreign Area Fellowship of the US Social Science Research Council, supplemented by a grant from the Radcliffe-Brown Fund of the Association of Social Anthropologists. Subsequent visits to Peru were supported by the UK Social Science Research Council, the Nuffield Foundation, and the Staff Research Fund of the London School of Economics.

1   Many towns and cities in Peru boast miraculous crucifixes commemorating major earthquakes, to which the country is notoriously prone. The most famous is El Señor de Los Milagros in Lima, whose annual fiesta is similarly the occasion for a national civic parade, frequently attended by the president of the republic himself.
2   Mary and Christ, to the best of my knowledge, never appear together in the same shrine set.

REFERENCES

Avila, F. de (1598) *Dioses y Hombres de Huarochirí* trans. José María Arguedas, Lima: Museo Nacional de Historia/Instituto de Estudios Peruanos, 1966.
Christian, W. A. (1972) *Person and God in a Spanish Valley*, New York: Academic Press.
———— (1981) *Local Religion in Sixteenth-Century Spain*, Princeton: Princeton University Press.
Kubler, G. (1946) 'The Quechua in the colonial world', in J. H. Steward (ed.) *Handbook of South American Indians Vol. 2: The Andean Civilizations*, Washington, DC: Bureau of American Ethnology.
Morinis, E. A. (1984) *Pilgrimage in the Hindu Tradition: A Case Study of West Bengal*, Oxford University South Asian Series, Delhi: Oxford University Press.

Pfaffenberger, B. (1979) 'The Kataragama pilgrimage: Hindu–Buddhist inter-action and its significance in Sri Lanka's polyethnic social system', *Journal of Asian Studies* 38: 253–70.

Sallnow, M. J. (1974) 'La peregrinación andina', *Allpanchis* 7: 101–42.

_____ (1981) 'Communitas reconsidered: the sociology of Andean pilgrim-age', *Man* 16: 163–82.

_____ (1982) 'A trinity of Christs: cultic processes in Andean Catholicism', *American Ethnologist* 9: 730–49.

_____ (1987) *Pilgrims of the Andes: Regional Cults in Cusco*, Washington, DC: Smithsonian Institution Press.

_____ (1990) 'Dual cosmology and ethnic division in an Andean pilgrimage cult', in N. R. Crumrine and E. A. Morinis (eds) *Pilgrimage in Latin America*, New York: Greenwood Press.

Vrijhof, P. H. (1979) 'Official and popular religion in 20th century Christianity', in P. H. Vrijhof and J. D. J. Waardenburg (eds) *Official and Popular Religion: Analysis of a Theme for Religious Studies*, The Hague: Mouton.

Index

Rabinow, P. 3, 28,
'redemptive mission', Israel's 119
Redfield, R. 4, 29
religion and polity 131–4
Rinschede, G. 34, 50
Rue du Bac (Paris) 43–4

sacred, perception of the 9–16;
    miraculous 20, 22–5, 31, 125,
    139; sacrificial 22, 60–5, 71
St Bernadette *see* Lourdes
St Pé (France) 45
St Saviour's friary 114
Sallnow, Michael J. 1–27, 29, 75, 76,
    78, 97, 153
San Giovanni Rotondo 1–2, 12–13,
    14–15, 17, 19–20, 77–95; about
    pilgrimage 78–9; the culting of
    Pio 83–4; maps 82, 85; Pio's
    charitable works 81–3; Pio's
    material legacy 87–9; Pio's
    spiritual legacy 89–90, 96; Pio's
    time in 80–1; the sacred
    transformed 90–1; the town today
    84–7; the 'true message' of Pio
    89, 91–4
Sarakatsani, the 111
Señor de Los Temblores shrine
    (Andes) 143, 146
Señor de Qoyllur Rit'i shrine (Andes)
    12, 143, 144
Señor de Wank'a shrine (Andes) 12,
    16, 21, 23, 25, 26, 144, 146
Seventh Day Adventists 47
Sharma, J. 5, 28
shrines, Andean 139–46; map 140
shrines, the rise of 124–7
sick pilgrims 16–24, 45–8; and
    healing 55–9 *see also* Blessed
    Sacrament procession
sidhasthanaya see Sinhala
Sinhala (Sri Lanka) 2, 4, 5, 7, 8, 17,
    23, 122–34; map of Sri Lankan
    shrines 123; person-centred
    shrines 127–9; religion and polity
    131–4; the rise of pilgrimage
    shrines 124–7; shift from place to
    person 129–31

Skultans, V. 16, 29
Soubirous, Bernadette 52, 55
'spatialization of charisma' *see*
    sacred, perceptions of the
Spiro, M. 3, 29
Srinivas, M. N. 4, 29
stagiaires see Hospitality of Our
    Lady of Lourdes
stigmata 80–1, 90–1
Stirrat, R. L. 2, 14, 29, 122–34, 136
suffering body, the, in Catholic and
    Protestant discourses 16–24,
    46–8; in pilgrimages 45–6 *see
    also* holism
Sumption, J. 21, 25, 29
Suvagama shrine (Sri Lanka) 127–8,
    130–1, 134
Syllabus of Errors (Pius IX) (1864) 32
symbolic exchange 24–6

Talawila shrine (Sri Lanka) 124–7,
    129, 130
Talbot-Rice, D. 119, 121
Talbot-Rice, T. 119, 121
Temple Foundation, the (Jerusalem)
    119
textual pilgrimage 1, 8–9, 14; and
    Jerusalem 99–108
titulaires see Hospitality of Our Lady
    of Lourdes
Tiwanaku shrine (Andes) 138
Turner, B. S. 20, 29
Turner, E. 4–5, 29, 52, 76, 78, 130,
    136
Turner, V. W. 4–5, 29, 52, 76, 78,
    130, 136

Ullmann, W. 105, 121

Van der Veer, P. 5, 29, 95, 97
varam (delegated authority) *see*
    patronage, Sri Lankan
Vatican II (Second Vatican Council)
    10, 35, 130
vernacular language, use of 70
Virgin of Czestochowa (Poland) 26
Virgin of Medjugorje (Yugoslavia) 26
Vogel, C. 107, 121